Dr. Alu

The Speaker's Commentary [The Holy Bible, Ed. by F.C. Cook]

This Book Will make any Believer of God and the Bible So angry you will Wont to throw it away.

Dr. alvius Lavon Womack

1st Corintheans 1:21-25

1st Corintheans 2:7

Ephesians 3:10-11

THE

SPEAKER'S COMMENTARY;

REVIEWED

BY

THOMAS LUMISDEN STRANGE,

LATE A JUDGE OF THE HIGH COURT OF MADRAS, AND AUTHOR OF " THE BIBLE
IS IT THE WORD OF GOD?"

LONDON:

N. TRÜBNER & CO., 60 PATERNOSTER ROW.

1871.

101. f. 342

PREFACE.

IN the struggle maintained to free the world from
the bondage of a system conceived upon the appall-
ing view that our great Creator is other than our
universal friend, it is an inestimable advantage when
the defenders of the faith invaded can be made to
show their hand. There is a commotion in their
camp not to be mistaken. A Revision Company are
occupied in patching up the "Word of God," pulling
out here, putting in there, re-translating it in portions,
in the hope that its challenged foundations may be
made securer than they are. Dignitaries of the highest
order enter the pulpit to put down "infidelity." A
select society is formed to disseminate lectures with
the same view. And now a most important body
come forward with their commentary to clear the
word of its imputed errors. Such an effort, we have
the right to suppose, is the best that could be made

under permitting circumstances. All that can be commanded by learning, zeal, and concert of judgment, shaped upon the many similar efforts that have foregone, must, we may believe, be here combined. And the weight of names, with the dignities attaching thereto, is to give a solid assurance to the whole. Nothing therefore can be more acceptable to those whose object it is to sift out these views than to have them stated in this comprehensive and authoritative manner.

But is it a compliment to any work that it should require this elaborate support? Truth ordinarily commends itself by the presence of inherent force, and does not need any peculiar extraneous elucidation. And if an author's meaning is not apparent, the fact is the reverse of favourable to him. Surely a word from God, directed, in all ages, to the heads and hearts of men of every grade and stamp, needed for their guidance, important to their "salvation," should reveal itself by unassisted luminosity as a ray of sunshine. It is when there is an absence of lucidity, an appearance of error, a defect of information, an obsoleteness of matter, that the aid of a commentator is called for, and the circumstance assuredly is against the perfection of the work requiring his supporting hand. An apologetic tone, a system of defensive artifice, betrays the weakness of whatever has to be so sustained. All commentaries are cast in this shape, and it is a form, in fact, to which every Biblicist is driven when followed up in argument. Most painful is it to observe shifts such as these when the matter dealt with is alleged to be unerring truth derived from God.

There was a time when men were burnt for their opinions, or otherwise persecuted. Commentaries were then unnecessary. The arm of power was the sufficient substitute. Afterwards, as gradually the concession to exercise thought was forced from the repressors, doubts and difficulties arose, and had to be solved rationally, and commentaries made their appearance. The teachers then knew but little, and those to be taught were alike innocent of information. It was just the era for successful commentaries. Whatever required to be said, could be said, the means of refutation being wanting. But from that stage we have passed to one of fast accumulating knowledge, and the time for commentaries—favourable ones,— is passing away. The gentlemen before us labour, perceptibly, under the difficulties of the altered position. Their possible hearers know much, and they them-

selves are, doubtless, equally well informed. Knowledge is ordinarily power, but here it is weakness.
The sense the commentators have of the strength
accruing on the other side hampers them sadly.
They are driven to manifest evasions, and palpable
admissions, all most damaging to the cause undertaken.
The battle is lost at the first clash of arms.

This is just the opportunity their adversaries have
sought for. A Fabian policy might prolong the
struggle. But a front maintained at Sedan is all
we want.

GREAT MALVERN, *November* 1871.

CONTENTS.

THE SPEAKER'S COMMENTARY.

———◆———

THE HOLY BIBLE, with an Explanatory and Critical
Commentary, by Bishops and other Clergy of the
Anglican Church. Edited by F. C. COOK, M.A.,
Canon of Exeter.—JOHN MURRAY.

WE have at length an instalment of a work which *The provok-ing cause.*
many have been looking for with something resembling
impatient expectation. It is designed to fill an important place, and to supply a very decided need.
The world, or at least that portion of the world which
alone is worth speaking of, namely, the Christian
portion, and more especially that section of the Christian community known to be apostolically, and therefore divinely, constituted, because established by law,
were a few years ago scandalised by a spectacle of
unusual, and, in fact, unexampled occurrence — a
spectacle so much out of the course of experience,
that we should have said it could not have happened,
had it not, in fact, taken place. A dignitary of the
church we refer to, one sent to overlook or episcopize
a distant dependency of her Majesty's realm, ventur-
ing one day beyond the proper limits of his official
functions, entered into conversation, and, we are sorry
to say, discussion, with one of the ignorant, unen-
lightened, and unchristianized inhabitants of the land.

A

The savage, untaught to bow to authority, especially to such an authority as was then addressing him, ventured to exercise his own uninstructed mind over the matters presented to him, not for consideration or investigation, but for belief. The Bishop thought to tread upon his toes ecclesiastically, and to fix him upon the spot on which it was desirable he should stand. The savage, irreverently, and probably designedly, introduced his pedal terminations under the Bishop's sole, and absolutely unsettled him in his foundations. The Bishop did the last thing one in his position should have dreamt of doing. He went home, and, without depending upon his St Jerome, his St Augustine, or his St Chrysostom, pursued the line of thought to which the savage had introduced him. The poison necessarily worked. The Bishop's system became unepiscopized. Feeling the circlets of his mitre pressing upon his brows, and restraining thought, or at least free thought, he laid it aside. His robes impeded his progress. These he tucked up. His lawn sleeves embarrassed his action, and he rolled them back. Then, forgetting what he really was, he went to work, we regret to say, like a man. Not checked by any sense of the inviolability of the sacred precincts of which he was an appointed guardian, he absolutely set himself to undermine the very edifice he had to· sustain. He proceeded to examine its foundations, rudely pulling aside the surface stones, and bringing to view the rubbish that had been thrust behind them. Some foreign workmen guided him to the weaker points, and he made rapid advances in his unhallowed expositions. Unfortunately he worked with only too great results, worthless though, to well-disciplined minds, such results are, and must ever be.

He enlarged his cavities, and others, encouraged in the evil course of judging for themselves, looked in and observed the vacancy beyond. His course had previously been taken by others engaged like himself to sustain the sacred building. A band of these had clubbed together in their "essays" to cultivate the forbidden exercise of thought over what has already been thought out for us officially, apostolically, and consequently divinely. Recently a small but spirited member of the genus prop, with sling and stone, like a stripling of old, bent on the overthrow of giants, has chosen to step out in the line of illicit freedom, unrestrained by the thirty and nine shackles carefully placed round his ankles when he was first allowed to exercise his movements ; and he, eager, active, and self-reliant, has made fearful advances, of course all in the wrong direction, so as actually to have incurred the unspeakable calamity of having the door of the edifice shut in his face, when he would still, though fond of freedom, have abided within its honoured walls.

The work of which we have the first portions before us is designed to correct and prevent these fatal liberties. It is to bring us back to the good old ways, to settle every doubt, to remove every scruple, and to give us ready answers wherewith to meet the adversaries—our reasons for the faith which at all events should be in us, if not actually so.

The suggestion, strange to say, of undertaking such a work, did not come from the guardians of the flock, but from one of the flock itself. This, however, was a bell-wether, no less a personage than the Speaker of our great legislative assembly—in this instance the spokesman of the whole disturbed community. He

The motive power.

saw the danger a-head, and how to meet it, and rousing, we apprehend with some little difficulty, the shepherds to a sense of their duty, has been the means of arming us with the valuable results now presented to us.

The machinery.   The work in question will no doubt be known familiarly as the *Speaker's Commentary.* It is the combined effort of the Archbishop of York, the Bishops of Ely, of Bath and Wells, of St David's, of Chester, of London, and of Derry and Raphoe, and thirty others of the clergy—a body of Right Reverends, Very Reverends, Venerables, and Reverends, headed by their Most Reverend leader, labouring to uphold the divine authority of the Bible against the incursions of Bishop Colenso and the disciples of free-thought. The sheep will at all events be satisfied with the number, and the potential titles, of those who have come to their defence, whatever may prove ultimately to be the issue of their labours.

The portions before us embrace the Pentateuch, and therefore include the chief strongholds that have been attacked—the authorship of Moses, the creation, fall, deluge, and exodus. We will put what restraint we can upon our admiring faculties, and in limits as restricted as our feelings will allow, endeavour to give some idea of the success with which our learned, reverend, and very reverend advisers, have prosecuted the pleasant task committed to them.

Inspiration.   The first question is of course the divine origination of the Bible, how the Deity came into contact with and inspired his human instruments. On this matter the reverend commentators observe a prudent silence. It was a contact which no one could have witnessed or have described. It was one of which probably the instrument himself was unconscious. The only way of establishing such a fact is therefore to assume it, and this the reverend gentry have done. And so tenacious are they of the position, that they allow no considerations, no incongruities, no admitted presence of elements foreign to and independent of the alleged divine elements, to disturb it. Of this we shall have ample evidence as we advance in our examination.

Of the actuality of the inspiration, the divine light illuminating and shining out of the inspired author, we have one, and, as far as we have observed, but one direct example, and it is an illustration beautiful in its simplicity. It is also, as a work of God should be, wide in its comprehensiveness. We notice it, not only as a solitary instance of the kind, but as one, we apprehend, that hitherto must have been overlooked.

We refer to the notable declaration of the meekness of Moses appearing in Num. xii. 3. We have always had some degree of difficulty in recognizing this feature in the character of the great Hebrew legislator, disturbed, as he is occasionally shown to have been, by little ebullitions ; as when he took the law into his own hands, or rather went against the law, and killed the Egyptian ; when he dashed the sacred stones, written upon "with the finger of God," to pieces on the ground ; and when, at the water of Meribah, he lost his temper, and therewith his inheritance. Nor were we the better satisfied of his title to the character, in that he stood indebted for it to his own pen. Commentators, that is the unlicensed ones, have, in fact, been in the habit of considering the occurrence of the passage to be one, amongst other evidences, that Moses could not himself have been the author of the record in which it appears. However, we are now set right.

"*The man Moses was very meek.* These words have been, with no little insensibility to the finer traits of the passage, often regarded as words which Moses himself could not have penned; and accordingly have been cited sometimes as indicating an interpolation, sometimes as proof that the book is not Mosaic. When we regard them as uttered by Moses not '*proprio motu*,' but under the direction of the Holy Spirit which was upon him (cf. xi. 17), they exhibit a certain 'objectivity' which is a witness at once to their genuineness and also to their inspiration" (I. 693).

Thus, with a stroke of his pen, by taking the unusual step of self-laudation, Moses establishes his own authorship, and at the same time his inspired power. It may not be thought superfluous to have provided an engine of seven and thirty clergy power to drag us to such a conclusion.

The inspired materials. We come now to the composition of the work, the materials of which it is made up—a consideration somewhat strange to our uninstructed minds, which would have led us to suppose that a writer, with the Omniscient at his side to prompt and supply him, would have proved adequate to every occasion, and not have required to lean upon earlier human labourers for his inspired knowledge. In fact, it becomes difficult, in a work so put together, compositely, to see exactly where the scope remains for the intervention of the divine dictator. But this is not all. The sacred record, after being issued by its inspired author, has not passed down to us without being subjected, as any common human production might be, to the operations—"recension" is the word carefully selected—of an editor. It is in this way added to, illustrated, and, in a word,

improved upon, and by one who had the advantage of
living at a period nine hundred years removed from
the occurrences over which he exercised his revising
pen. It is devoutly to be hoped that he did not let
modern matter, picked up anyhow, displace that which
was ancient, genuine, and divine ; that he was modest
in his interferences with the word as it had come out
from the Almighty ; and, prominently, that he was
guarded in not introducing accomplished facts, known
of to himself, as prophetic utterances of the original
author. We feel that we are treading upon danger-
ous ground, and wish we could have been assured, as
some indeed, seeing the need, have not hesitated to
assert was the case, that the " recensor " was himself
inspired. But we must let the Commentary speak for
itself. The circuitous candour of its acknowledgments
will be observable.

"It is not necessary to insist, that every word of the
Pentateuch was written down by the hand of Moses in his
own autograph. He may have dictated much, or all of it,
to Joshua, or to some secretary or scribe. . . . It is not
necessary to deny that the Pentateuch, though the work of
the great Prophet and Lawgiver whose name it bears, may
have undergone some recension in after times, as by Ezra
or others. . . . If Ezra collated MSS. and carefully edited
the books of Moses, it is not impossible, and is not inconsistent with the original authorship, that he should have admitted explanatory notes, which some think (rightly or
wrongly) to betray a post-Mosaic hand. . . . It is not necessary to deny that Moses had certain documents or traditions referring to the patriarchal ages, which he incorporated
into his history. Indeed, it is likely that such traditions
should have come down through Shem and Abraham to
Joseph and the Israelites in Egypt. And there can be no

reason why an inspired historian should not have worked up such trustworthy materials into the history of his people." (I. 2.)

Deuteronomy

The character of the last section of the Pentateuch, entitled significantly Deuteronomy, has always presented difficulties, in that this book goes over ground already traversed in the prior portions, and with divergencies. The Commentary admits the fact, but not, of course, to the discredit of the record.

"Deuteronomy is an authoritative and inspired commentary on the law; serving in some respects also as a supplement and codicil to it. . . . . . Various texts from the book have been adduced as proofs that it was not composed by the author of the books preceding it. These contain deviations from the earlier narrative, additions to it, or assumed inconsistencies with it. . . . . . No doubt, some of these are important, and require careful consideration and explanation."

Then, arguing that "a forger would certainly have anxiously removed all such seeming discrepancies as those in question," it is added,

"The very occurrence then of the phenomena in question, arising on a comparison of Deuteronomy with Exodus, Leviticus, and Numbers, striking as those phenomena are, and just because they are striking, is a *prima facie* token of authenticity. No one but the original legislator and historian would deal with his subject in this free and independent spirit."

The particular divergencies referred to, are, as to the appropriation of tithes, a subject on which we should have expected a more sensitive manifestation of feeling on the part of clerical brethren than is displayed; the failure to distinguish between the functions of the priests, the sons of Aaron, and the Levites at large—

also a tender subject; and "the total omission of large portions of the Sinaitic legislation." And there is an "interweaving" of archæological and topographical remarks, which are seen to be "insertions made by a later reviser, perhaps a much later reviser, after the book was complete." Footnotes, it appears, were not then invented, and editors were in the habit of incorporating their remarks with the original texts.

"Hence it is on the whole not unlikely that the passages in question were, as Prideaux long ago maintained, see 'Connection' (Part I., Book v., §§ 3 and 4), glosses added by Ezra, who would certainly regard himself as fully authorised thus to interpolate. But the question as to the Mosaic authorship of the book is not affected by any conclusion which may be formed about such isolated passages." (I. 792, 796-799.)

We are here forcibly reminded of the criticism on the declaration by Moses of his otherwise imperceptible and inappreciable meekness. That unusual exhibition was an evidence both of his authorship and his inspiration. And exactly thus the present divergencies from the prior statements are so many tokens of authenticity. Being of this value, it is a pity even that they were not multiplied; but we must not be greedy of proofs when enough, under inspired guidance, are afforded for demonstration. The want of accord between the terms of the ten commandments appearing in Exod. xx. 8-17, as compared with Deut. v. 12-21, is of course in the same way demonstrative that we have here the exact transcript of the very words of God. Under the able manipulations of our reverend friends, blemishes become beauties, and the overthrowings of adversaries stable supports. We have also the remarkable phenomenon of inspiration

Proofs of authenticity.

on inspiration, the "inspired commentary" on the inspired text, followed up, strangely enough, by the improving hands of human editors, guessed at, or unknown. Would that we could think that the present glosses of our reverend authors were of the same exalted character as the Deuteronomic commentary! Surely, if this feature does not belong to them, it cannot, in the divine providence, be needed for our edification and absolute safety.

We have then a whole chain of acknowledgements from other sources.

ifice.   Sacrifice is a most important ordinance.

"A Hebrew sacrifice, like a christian sacrament, possessed the inward and spiritual grace, as well as the outward and visible sign."

We would rather that the statement had been made more absolutely. What if the christian sacraments should prove wanting in that which is here required for the Hebrew sacrifice? We have always, we must confess, found a difficulty in discerning the actuality of the regeneration of a squalling infant when brought to the baptismal font, or the divine presence in the baked and fermented elements. This must be, we fear, owing to the want in us of the "spiritual insight," spoken of further on, which conveyed, to which, or to how many of the Hebrew community we wish we had been told, "lessons in the symbols of the altar," "converging with more or less distinctness towards the Lamb slain from the foundation of the world" (I. 495). We wonder with what measure of absence of distinctness the perception of this great "mystery" "which was kept secret since the world began" (Rom. xvi. 25), is compatible. We, however, give this account of the ordinance of sacrifice, as we say, just to point to the exceeding importance of the institution. But when we ask whence came the ordinance, we are drawn to an unexpected and somewhat embarrassing conclusion.

"There has been in all times a difference of opinion as to the divine or human origin of sacrifice. . . . There is a deep silence as to any such command, whilst the institution of the Sabbath and of other positive ordinances is distinctly recorded. Hence, many have thought that sacrifice was dictated by an instinct of natural religion, and then, by a condescension to man's infirmity, sanctioned for a temporary purpose, and constituted an image of redemption" (I. 53).

We have been accustomed to suppose that natural instincts could avail naught among a race of beings formed to be dependent for their religious perceptions, and methods of access to the Almighty, on inspired records. But we are bound to recognise the indication of our preceptors, who appear to discern in human inventiveness the origin of the divinely adopted ordinance of sacrifice. The first man born into the world resorted to the rite; so it is said; and he must have done so in a natural, and not an inspired way, as he failed to gain acceptance of his act. It is true his was not a blood sacrifice, but his brother's was, and the origin for both must have been the same. Beyond this we would not go of ourselves. If the ordinance has received the sanction of God, we would rather depend for this conclusion on our commentators.

The same as to the rite of circumcision. This also was an important ordinance. It distinguished the chosen people from the outcast and abandoned world at large. Herodotus, our friends notice, says, "The Egyptians and Ethiopians had it from the most

Circumcision.

remote antiquity, so that he cannot tell which had it first." Egyptologists have traced its prevalence to the time of the fourth dynasty, that is, " from at least 2400 B.C.; therefore much before the date generally assigned to Abraham, B.C. 1996," and have found "that it was not confined to the priests, as is, they say, learned from the mummies and the sculptures, where circumcision is made a distinctive mark between the Egyptians and their enemies." For these statements the very orthodox Wilkinson, as also Rawlinson, are cited. " If this be correct," it is added, " we must conclude . . . . that the Divine command was not intended to teach a new rite, but to consecrate an old one into a sacramental ordinance." So far there was the same system as in the divine adoption of the human device of sacrifice. But here our commentators exhibit some little reluctance to rest upon the conclusion presented to them. They would rather, if it might be permitted them, discredit Herodotus and the interpretation of the hieroglyphics, and suppose it possible that Joseph may have introduced the rite among the Egyptians (I. 121, 122). It is certainly a mark of deep penetration, and of considerable boldness, to arrive at such a result without a datum; but with the numerous other instances apparent of the adaptation of the divine to the human mind, allowed to have prevailed, we confess we are unable to see why this introduction of circumcision into the inspired code should give rise to any special difficulty.

Our commentators are good enough to point out a multitude of these adaptations.

The cherubim.
There are the cherubim, the effigies of which were on the lid of the ark, on the curtains of the tabernacle, on the walls and doors of the temple, and on

objects in use in the temple. The offices of the creatures represented appear to have been " to guard what is sacred and unapproachable," as the gate of paradise, the ark, with the tables of the law therein, "to surround the mystic throne of God and to attend his presence," "perhaps to bear up the throne of God upon their wings, and to carry him when he appeared in his glory," as it is said, " He rode upon a cherub, and did fly." Some of them have six wings, as in Isaiah vi. 2, where the appellation is Seraphim, — two for covering the face, two to cover the feet, and two to use in flying. Some have only four, as in Ezek. i. 8. They are provided, moreover, " each " with " four faces, viz., of a man, of a lion, of an ox, of an eagle," as in Ezek. i. 10 ; x. 14. In Rev. iv. 8 they are exhibited " with six wings, having eyes all over." This we should have thought particularly inconvenient. These are certainly formidable animals, the rencontre with which would not be pleasant, especially to the weaker, who are also the most devout sex. Whence these have been derived is happily well known.

"Mr Layard . . . . discovered in Nineveh gigantic winged bulls with human heads, winged lions, and human figures with hawk or eagle heads, corresponding nearly with the winged cherubim of Ezekiel and St John. These gigantic figures are generally placed as guards or sentinels at the entrances of temples and palaces, like the guarding cherubim of Holy Writ. Moreover, they are evidently not objects of idolatrous worship, but appear rather as worshippers than as divinities."

Then, noticing that Mr Layard did not consider the objects in question to be of great antiquity, the commentators add

" Far more likely is it that some Egyptian type should have been followed; and we find in the Egyptian sculptures, and in the 18th dynasty, which was probably the dynasty of the Exodus, examples of a shrine or ark wonderfully calculated to remind us of the ark of the covenant made by Moses. It is carried by persons of the sacerdotal race, by staves, as the Levites carried the ark. In the centre is the symbol of the Deity, and two winged human figures spread out their wings around and over it " (Lepsius ' Denkm' III. Bl. 14).

Ezekiel, we are reminded, had his visions "by the river Chebar, in the land of the Chaldeans; and there he and his people would, no doubt, have become familiarized with the gigantic winged guardians of the temples and the palaces in Babylonia and Assyria, the bulls and lions, and eagle-headed men, and human-headed bulls. . . . . In God's dealings with man, he constantly uses for lessons things just before men's eyes. And so he may have done in this case with Ezekiel. . . . . To Moses, on the other hand, but still on the same principle, God had dictated the carving of figures like those which he had seen in Egypt, figures emblematical of guardianship, and of the reverence of those who wait constantly upon God, but which had never been objects of idolatrous worship. Thus he sanctioned, or at least tolerated, that which seems so dear to religious humanity," "the use of symbolism, where dangers from its abuse were not great" (I. 50-52).

We do not understand the phrase, "religious humanity." Can there be any thing really worthy to be called religious without inspiration ?

We confess to some little difficulties connected with this portion of the exposition, the solution of which is doubtless only non-apparent to us because of our own ignorance, or it may be obtuseness. We see it said that Ezekiel described what he saw in Chaldea, and Moses what he was familiar with in Egypt. Probably the representation in the text that Ezekiel drew from likenesses in heaven—"Now it came to pass," mentioning the precise date of the occurrence, "as I was among the captives by the river of Chebar, that the heavens were opened, and I saw visions of God" (i. 1), and the statement that Moses modelled from "patterns of things in the heavens" (Heb. viii. 5; ix. 23), are divergencies, which, if properly estimated, would turn out to be additional proofs, beyond those already put before us, of the scope, and, in fact, the unlimited range, of an inspired understanding. And we think it must be so, because again we have a beautiful conflict between St. Paul's recognition of the following of the patterns in heaven, and the command to the Jews not to make "any graven image, or any likeness of any thing that is in heaven above, or that is' in the earth beneath, or that is in the water under the earth," which we do not know how otherwise to account for. Then, as we go round the subject to another side, we are not quite sure, from what our expositors say, whether the objects in question have deen drawn from realities, or were merely vagaries of puerile Pagan fancy. We would prefer of course that the former should be the case, but, if so, it would be necessary that the Pagan delineators should have had access, somehow, to the originals. It is quite possible that favoured individuals, unknown to us, and perhaps unconsciously to themselves, may have been taken secretly into heaven, as was St. Paul (2 Cor. xii. 2), or, if that was too great a favour to be shown to heathens, caught up by some spirit by the hair of the head, as was Ezekiel (viii. 3), or it might be by the heels, and taken sufficiently near to see their models. This perhaps

[margin note, handwritten:] II Corinthians 12:1—4

would settle all difficulties. The heathen drew
from heavenly realities, and Moses and Ezekiel drew
from them, so that the "patterns" were truly heavenly although obtained from the heathen. The
"mystic throne of God" is an expression we should
have wished made clearer to us. Of course this does
not require that the throne was not a real one, nor
truly borne up on the wings of the ox &c. headed
animals. The sight would no doubt present a marvellous aspect, but then the whole sacred volume deals,
from one end to the other, from paradise to the celestial
but movable Jerusalem, in the marvellous, and as we feel
our expositors design us to accept the inspired description as a reality, we are prepared to do so. We could
have wished that it was not necessary to decide that
the objects copied from were not such as the heathen
put to idolatrous use. We certainly have seen, some-
where, delineations of a ram-headed Kneph, a bull-
headed Osiris or Serapis, a hawk-headed Horus, a dog-
headed Anubis, &c., gods worshiped by those from
whom Moses derived his images; and we notice that
our expositors recognise in the "two-winged human
figures" over the Egyptian ark, which was the model
of the sacred Hebrew ark, representations of "the
goddess Ma, under the two-fold notion of 'justice'
and 'truth'" (I. 51). This characteristic of the models
being Pagan idols, supposing it is admissible, can be
but a deepening of a blemish enhancing merit when
converted into what is beautifying.

Hobab.

We have ventured thus to play Hobab to our expositors' pillar of cloud and pillar of fire. These heavenly beacons were among the things prevailing
among the heathen which the Divine being adopted
for the benefit of the Jews. "Fire and smoke" were

used by them in advance of their hosts, "as signals in their marches," and "the Lord himself," our expositors assure us, "did for the Israelites by preternatural means that which armies were obliged to do for themselves by natural means" (I. 305). Hobab was "instead of eyes," to the Hebrew host (Num. x. 31.)

" The divine guidance of the Pillar of the Cloud would not render superfluous the human conductor who would indicate the spots where water, fuel, and pasture might be found, the dangers from hurricanes, and the localities infested by robbers." (I. 687).

We trust that it never so happened that the cloud indicated one direction, and Hobab another. This is a liberty, it will be observed, whatever our inclinations, we never venture to take with the indications of our expositors. No. Such conflict was easily avoidable. "Probably," they proceed to say, "the pillar prescribed only the general direction of the journey." The pillar evidently acted the part of commander, and Hobab was the quarter-master.

The other instances of divine legislation based upon human and Pagan rites and ordinations, noticed by our friends, are "the distinction of clean and unclean meats;" the "priesthood by inheritance;" "the priests shaving their whole bodies;" their "purification" by "bathing continually;" their use of "none but linen garments;" "the anointing of Aaron when clothed in his priestly robes," which "has an exact parallel in the Egyptian sculptures, where the king is anointed, clothed in royal robes, and with cap and crown on his head;" "the ceremony of the scapegoat;" the mysterious "Urim and Thummim on the breast of the high priest;" "the writing of the commandments of God on the door-posts and gates;"

Divine imitative originality.

B

"the erecting pillars and coating them with plaster to prepare for inscriptions" (I. 15, 16); "the lex leviratus," or "law of marriage with a brother's widow" (I. 198); "the putting off the shoes" when treading on "holy ground" (I. 261); the "uncleanness ascribed to childbirth" (I. 558); the "uncleanness from secretions" (I. 583); "the mode of slaughter" of animals sacrificially (I. 596); "the ordinance of the red heifer" (I. 651); "the trial of jealousy" (I. 669); the "shaving the head" of the "Nazarite" when he had accomplished the term of his vow (I. 673); the "fringes" that were to be on the borders of the Israelites' garments (I. 707); the "purification from the uncleanness of death" (I. 717); the use of "amulets" (I. 825).

The copyings are carried to an extent to have placed the elect people very much on the footing of the heathen, so that an Egyptian Hobab from the priesthood would have been the very one to guide them. Perhaps Moses was essentially such. He was trained in all the learning of "the wisdom of the Egyptians" (Acts vii. 22) for the first forty years of his life, purposely, no doubt, because of the divine appreciation of Egyptian rites, and design to adopt them for the model people. Our preceptors, however, say nothing as to this, and perhaps might repudiate the idea. The copying, in fact, we find to have been in some way, we suppose, unavoidable, for it appears, after all, to have been restricted to the narrowest bounds. "It seems wonderful," our commentators observe, "that there is so little in the sanctuary to remind us of any foreign association" (I. 434.) Little indeed! only the ark itself, and the effigies on its lid, and on the curtains, and the utensils; with the Urim and Thummim on the high priest's breast!

The difficulties to which so many have been subjected in judging of the Mosaic account of the creation are swept away by our commentators with brevity
and complete success. This, we confess, has afforded
unutterable relief to our own minds. Geology, we are
free to say, has disturbed us not a little. Moses tells
us of a chaos, followed by six successive acts of creation, occupying exactly one day each, after the ter-
mination of which, the great artificer, exhausted with
his labours, took that rest which his nature called for
during the course of another day, the seventh. This
day consequently became very holy, doing nothing
being characteristic of the Creator, while labour, as
many know, is a curse brought in by sin and Satan
at the fall. And so the Creator took his rest all
through the seventh day. What he did on the eighth,
we have never known, and have been afraid to ask.
Nor have we understood what the rest involved, beyond a cessation to create. It cannot have been such
rest as we mortals take, when, in nightly repose, we
cease from all action external to ourselves ; for, with
the Almighty withdrawn from attention to us, we
should all, we presume, have instantly ceased to be.
Such disturbing thoughts we have ever striven to
quell as invading the simplicity of the narrative, and
setting it against the realities around us. But geology stepped in with other matter, which we, in sooth,
could not so readily dispose of. A chaos has been
diligently looked for, and not found. But it may crop
up some day unexpectedly. The geologists insist
that, so far from the formlessness and void spoken of
by Moses, they have found layer upon layer, in an
appointed and never disturbed succession, filled with
curious remains, vegetable and animal, arranged with

the utmost regularity, as might be specimens in a cabinet. But then they have as yet looked but about fifteen miles below the earth's crust, and deeper down may lie the evidences of the chaos. Furthermore, they allege that the creations have been continuous and successive, one species replacing another, but all interlaced together in one uninterrupted course of operation, still apparently unconcluded. In this they point blank contradict Moses in his assertion of disconnected successional creation, each branch concluded in a day, and wound up with a seventh-day everlasting rest. And here it is that our commentators come to our inexpressible relief. The disturbing science, they tell us, is still too infantile to be worthy of notice (I. 63). Its uncertain prattlings need no reply. They will doubtless die off, and with maturer knowledge the babes may evince an orthodox turn, as many do in the progress of their studies.

The Sun. The Mosaic account, our commentators observe, commences with what was in the beginning. This we are told was the " beginning of all things," and therefore the sun then had his beginning, and it was the shining out of his light, and not his own formation, which occurred on the fourth day (I. 32). Here a world of difficulty is removed connected with the governance of the movements of the earth, the appearance of light, the occurrence of morning and evening, the ripening of grain and fruits, before and independently of the creation of the great orb from which all these processes result. But then, if the term " in the beginning" means "in the beginning of all things," and in these things the sun, how was it that all the rest of the creation found not their place among the "all things" of the beginning, so

that the remaining days, and their operations, might
have been dispensed with? This is a question, certainly, but it can require no answer, for our commentators give none. The light of the first day, as all
determine who hold this sort of view, was dim and·
murky. A dense atmosphere intervened, not allowing
the image of the sun to appear. Perhaps the "Revision Company" now at work in search for the
various readings with which the Bible happily abounds,
may find that God said on the first day, "Let there
be the sun, and there was the sun. And God saw the
light that it was bad;" and that on the fourth, he
merely "made the greater light to shine forth." For,
as we now read the text, if the light of the first day
was the light of the sun, and was "good," then we
have it shining forth as much on the first day as on
the fourth, and leave no special arrangement to be
carried out on the fourth day. If, again, there is no
such various reading, and the dilemma remains, we
feel satisfied that there is some way, known to our
commentators, and to be revealed by them hereafter,
of converting this blemish also into a beauty.

The geological deposits are sometimes termed the The record
record of the rocks, contrastedly with the Bible record, of the rocks.
both coming to us as testimonies from God. Our
commentators certainly do notice some difference
in the ordering of the arrangements between the two.
For example, terrestrial vegetation, according to
Moses, occurred on the third day, and marine animals
on the fifth; whereas the rocks exhibit the marine
products long before they show us the terrestrial.
If there is an error, it is certainly not on the part
of Moses, though the rocks undoubtedly are very
obstinate. Our commentators are not much arrested

here. They clear themselves of all by observing that this is "a difference not amounting to divergence" (I. 36). We wish the difference had been greater, for then they would evidently have been the more attracted by it, and have explained it altogether away.

The anti- quity of man.   "At present," they observe, "the greatest inconsistency alleged as between Genesis and science is to be found in the question of the antiquity of man." And therewith is their greatest success. They give a solution which, being admitted, is unanswerable.

"Whilst," they say, "there is at least good reason for withholding confident assent from the conclusions of some eminent geologists as to the evidence of the drift; it is quite possible to believe that Genesis gives us no certain data for pronouncing on the time of man's existence on the earth. The only arguments are to be drawn from the genealogies. As those given by the evangelists are confessedly incomplete, there cannot be sufficient reason for maintaining that those in Genesis must have been complete. It is true, that we have only conjecture to lead us here : but if the genealogies, before and after the Flood, present us only with the names of leading and 'representative' men ; we can then allow no small latitude to those who would extend the duration of man upon the earth to more than the commonly received six thousand years." (I. 30.)

This is exquisite. The acknowledged error of the gospels serves to set right the Mosaic record. Again blemishes become beauties, and if the argument requires strengthening, we have only to magnify the blemish. Say the six thousand years have to be lengthened to sixty thousand. Dr Bennet Dowler's estimate of the fossil man of the Mississippi requires 57,000 (Types of Mankind, p. 338). We need not hesitate to allow it. We stretch out the period by placing the genealogies so much the more in the wrong. We can with equal ease gain six hundred thousand years for man, and so on *ad infinitum.* As long as we possess the multiplication table we are safe. It is true, we acquire this liberty by setting "only conjecture" against revelation; but then revelation has very many aspects, and conjecture may hit upon the right one.

The susceptibilities of the genealogies are illustrated by the well-known divergencies between the three texts we are fortunate enough to possess. The lives of the Patriarchs, according to the Hebrew text, sum up 1656 years to the flood. The Samaritan version gives 1307, and the Septuagint, or Greek translation, which happens to be much more ancient than any of the originals, gives 2262 (I. 60). This, we are happy to find, "in no degree affects the veracity of the Sacred Record," and for the self-evident reason that falsehood always serves to demonstrate truth.

"It is well known that there have been some few designed corruptions in the text of the New Testament. It need not surprise us, therefore, if we find reason to think that there were some attempts of a like kind in the Old Testament."

This is encouraging, certainly.

"And though we believe in the divine guidance and inspiration of the original writer, we have no right to expect that a miraculous power should have so watched over the transmission of the records, as to have preserved them from all possible errors of transmission, though a special Providence may have guarded them from such loss or mutilation, as would have weakened their testimony to divine and spiritual truth" (I. 62).

This we quite understand. It was an object with God to have the original message rightly taken down. The Telegraph Office.

We will suppose this to be in the telegraph office of despatch.   In what shape it reached its destination,—that is, was transmitted to us, was not so important. We can answer for Moses, but perhaps not quite so certainly for Ezra and Co., who were the Reuters of that day; still less for the telegraph boys, who have actually brought the message to us. Boys always will be mischievous, even the educated portion of them, and these boys evidently could write.

For the sake of illustration we go back to our first citation on this subject, taken from page 30.   It continues thus ;—

"The appearance of completeness in the genealogies is an undoubted difficulty; yet perhaps not insuperable, when we consider all that may have happened (nowhere more probably than here) in the transmission of the text from Moses to Ezra, and from Ezra to the destruction of Jerusalem."

Reuter and Co. are not quite clear here; but, ah! those errand boys!   They not only tampered with the message, striking out portions thereof, but so arranged what remained as to make the damage apparently irreparable.   The book of Numbers exhibits the work of these parties, Reuter and Co. and the errand boys.

"It is likely indeed that this book, as others, underwent, after it left the hands of its composer, a revision, or perhaps more than one revision, in which here and there later elements were introduced. These, indeed, cannot have been of any great bulk."

Of course not.

". . . . The indications of interpolation in xiii., xiv., and xvi. are of another kind, and more convincing."

Some are here pointed out.

"These facts, as well as the repetitions and want of consecutiveness apparent in the chapters as they stand, render it likely that a later and independent, but not inconsistent account,"

(Inconsistent ! certainly not.)

" has been interwoven with the earlier one. . . . . Chapter xxxii. presents some similar characteristics to xiii. and xiv." (I. 653).

The question how we come to have the minute particulars of what was wrought by God in heaven and earth before any one of our race came into existence, is full of interest, and has not been overlooked. We are, in fact, rich enough to possess two such accounts, and both in the inspired volume. That in Gen. i., ii. 1-3

Traditionary sources.

" Was very probably the ancient primæval record of the formation of the world. It may even have been communicated to the first man in his innocence. At all events, it very probably was the great Semitic tradition, handed down from Noah to Shem, from Shem to Abraham, and from Abraham, through Isaac and Joseph, to the Israelites who dwelt in Egypt."

Probability is of course sufficient to satisfy us, at this distance of time, of an unascertainable fact. Our commentators are cautious enough not to say who made the communication to the first man. It may have been his wife, who, we know, held a conversation with a serpent, and so acquired knowledge. True and detailed though the particulars were, Moses was not satisfied therewith.

" Without interfering with the integrity of this (the first account), the sacred author proceeds in the same chapter to add a supplementary history, briefly recapitulating the history of creation, with some little addition (in vv. 4-7)" (I. 27).

It might even have been said variation. Where he got this second history is not suggested, but we should not be too inquisitive. We ought to be contented with the probability that the first account was traditionary, and that, not satisfied therewith, Moses picked up, somehow, another. The heathen, happily for them, have similar accounts. Of course Moses did not here condescend to draw from them, as he did so copiously, under divine instructions, in his efforts at legislation. The Zoroastrian account is particularly pointed to as exhibiting "important resemblance" to that in Scripture.

"The Persians," it seems, "of all people, except the Hebrews, were the most likely to have retained the memory of primitive traditions, and secondly, Zoroaster was probably brought into contact with the Hebrews, and with the prophet Daniel in the court of Darius, and may have learned much from such association" (I. 36).

This last idea we prize exceedingly, the times of Zoroaster, and we may add those of the author of the book of Daniel, being so certain.

The Fall.   The story of the Fall, we find, is part of that supplemental history which Moses added on to the primæval tradition of the creation (I. 27). The patriarchs, evidently, like other historians, were averse to lowering family reputation. They therefore did not hand down the great defeat to which their ancestors had been subjected in the rencontre with the serpent, of whom, consequently, they said nothing. This serves to warrant Moses's search for other information, ending, as we see, in his acquisition of it. Again the Zoroastrians, happy people, are found to have a similar record.

"The nearest resemblance, however, is traceable between the Biblical record and the teaching of the Zendavesta. As there is a likeness in the description of Paradise, so there is a special similarity in the account of the fall. According to the doctrine of Zoroaster, the first human beings, created by Ormuzd, the good principle, lived in a state of innocence in a happy garden with a tree which gave them life and immortality; but Ahriman, the evil principle, assuming the form of a serpent, offered them the fruit of a tree, which he had himself created ; they ate and became subject to evil, and to a continual contest between light and darkness, between the good motions of Ormuzd, and the evil suggestions of Ahriman. The theory that the Mosaic account was really borrowed from the Zoroastrian, . . . could only be established by proving that the early chapters of Genesis were not written till after the Babylonish captivity ; for it was then that the Jews first came into close contact with the Persians, and might have borrowed some of their superstitions." (I.48, 49.) They borrowed some things, it would seem, but certainly not this matter of the serpent. But here we are unwillingly reminded of the existence of Ezra, the "recensionist," or editor. Surely he could not have been the author, from unhallowed sources, of that additional narrative applied as an improvement to that of Moses, and Moses found to have been satisfied, after all, with the "primæval tradition," the dissatisfaction therewith being that of Ezra only! The idea is too unpleasant to be entertained for a moment ; nor can the interpolation by Ezra be actually proved. Still, if any choose, nevertheless, to dwell too pertinaciously on the identity of the two records, we may comfort ourselves by the thought that the Zoroastrians had access to the Patriarchs, and their traditions, equally with the Jews.

" If," our reverend advisers proceed to point out, " the legends of the Zendavesta were not borrowed by the Jews in their captivity, then the real contact point between them and the Jewish history must be found in pre-Mosaic times, in the days of the early patriarchs ; and then the fact, that the traditions of Persia were of all others the nearest to the Jewish traditions, may easily be explained " (I. 49).

This solution we personally much prefer to the other. It acquits Ezra, whom we wish with all our power to respect, of an unwarrantable but most important interpolation, and shows the borrower to have been Moses, upon whose inspired judgment we can implicitly rely. He found the " primæval tradition," as preserved by the Persians, to be more complete than that which had passed to him through his own ancestors, and so supplemented and improved his narrative. It was evidently one of those after thoughts, as when in Deuteronomy he wrote his inspired commentary on his earlier books.

The authenticity and inspiration of the narrative become thus clearly manifested, and in the characteristics of its style, we find that support to the conclusion which was to be expected. The unostentatious dignity with which the Bible stories are habitually conducted, carries with it the impress of their origin. Incidents of the most thrilling interest, fraught with the most stupendous consequences, are placed before us with all the simplicity of childhood. The facts may be wholly unexampled, and involve the overthrow of the settled laws of the creation, and yet are offered to us with that majestic consciousness of truth belonging to any current account of the most ordinary circumstances of the day. The contrast would become very apparent between what is conveyed by an inspired, or a mere human penman, were the latter permitted to tell in his own way one of these composedly given but startling tales. Let us make the essay.

THE SNAKE IN THE GRASS.

The Snake in the grass. *We once knew of a lovely woman, combining in her person youthfulness and maturity in a degree never attained before or*

*afterwards; not indebted to the arts of millinery for her at-
tractions—without temptation, in fact, to show herself otherwise than she was, being already happily disposed of in
matrimony to one on whom she had never set eyes before,
but who yet was the only man she could have accepted. Yes;
married was she at the early age of one second of time, without
consent of parents, for she had none. Strolling, a day or two
afterwards, in her husband's park, in a locality so secluded
that none have known where to find it, though its boundaries
are carefully laid down in the family archives; thinking of
nothing—how could she think? She was but an infant of
hours, so unripe in mental power as not to know good from
evil, without even a chance of cultivating such knowledge, there
being then no evil. All had been carefully examined by the
author of all things, and all had been found "very good."
Suddenly she perceives, gliding in the grass, a beauteous form.
Limbless, wingless, and yet not touching the ground with its
body, it moved with unimaginable ease, destitute of support.
Seeing the lovely female, this creature turned his piercing glance
upon her and arrested her attention. 'Fair one,' he said, 'are
you fond of fruit?' 'Surely,' she replied, 'I am fond of everything, for all is good. But what fruit is it that you speak
of?' 'That,' he said, describing it by name. 'That fruit,' she
replied, 'I am told I must not eat of, lest I die.' 'Of course you
understand what is meant by dying?' 'I know nothing,' she
answered, 'but that all is very good.' 'Then,' said the creature,
'take this fruit and eat it, for surely this also is very good.'
She little knew, poor thing, that in the midst of this beneficent
"very good" creation, here was one addressing her full of
subtlety, and that his speech teemed with lies, designed to effect
her ruin. In her infantine simplicity she took the good fruit
and ate of it, and gave thereof to her husband, equally simple
with herself. On this unutterable wrath fell upon them.
They were put under an everlasting ban, and driven from their
inheritance. An ox-headed monster was placed to guard its
portals, and they and their unborn progeny, for perpetual
generations, were turned into the outer world, consigned to*

Genesis 3:1-15

sufferings and the cold oblivion of death. A dim, shadowy, unpronounced, undiscernible, and very distant hope of deliverance, is thought by some to have been conveyed to them in the form of a curse upon the tempter ; and thus justice and mercy met together.

We wish to be pardoned this digression, and now return to our proper vocation.

Balaam's Ass.

Our commentators do not touch upon the phenomenon of the speaking serpent. This we regret, as it is a circumstance so often cavilled at, and the evidence thereof might, perhaps, under their able treatment, have been put on as satisfactory a footing as that which they have secured for Balaam's gifted donkey.

" The account of this occurrence," they observe, " can hardly have come from any one else than Balaam himself, and may perhaps have been given by him to the Israelites after his capture in the war against Midian ; cf. on 31. 8. That which is here recorded was apparently perceived by him alone amongst human witnesses. For though his two servants were with him (v. 22), and the envoys of Balaak also (v. 35), yet the marvel does not appear to have attracted their attention. The cries of the ass would seem, then, to have been significant to Balaam's mind only (so St Greg. Nyss. ' de Vita Mosis,' *sub finem*). God may have brought it about that sounds uttered by the creature after its kind became to the prophet's intelligence as though it addressed him in rational speech. . . . . On the other hand, the opinion that the ass actually uttered with the mouth articulate words of human speech (though still defended by Baumgarten, Von Gerlach, Words. &c.) ; or even that the utterance of the ass was so formed in the air as to fall with the accents of man's voice on Balaam's ears (a Lapide *in loc.*), seems irreconcileable with Balaam's behaviour. . . . . It seems scarcely conceivable that he could actually have heard human speech from the mouth of his own ass, and even go on as narrated in vv. 29, 30, to hold a dialogue with her, and show no signs of dismay and astonishment" (I. 736).

Perhaps we have here the origin of language, and this in connection with the Darwinian theory of the transmutation of species. The ass uttered the sounds proper to him as an ass, but wishing to be understood, he threw into them that will-power lying at the root of the law of physical progression, and the sounds fell upon the ear of the prophet addressed, as human language. What language? it will be asked. He-bray and Hebrew. The thing seems almost certain.

But to turn to the criticism of our friends. Its candour will commend itself to all sides. It might have fallen from the lips of Bishop Colenso, or any other objector. And its result is to establish the integrity of the record. Balaam had his impressions. Moses, who was a competent judge, considered them to be well-founded, and so set them down as facts. St Peter, another inspired man, was so satisfied of the fidelity of the imitative sounds in question, that he coincides with Moses in describing them as a reality; and he intensifies the marvel by accounting the ass, while "speaking with man's voice," to have been nevertheless a "dumb ass" (2 Pet. ii. 16). He might certainly have been cited in support of Baumgarten, &c. Perhaps the ascription of the dumbness made Baumgarten the more reliable of the two. Balaam was in every way a man to be respected, and the confidence placed in him by the inspired writers is amply warrantable.

"It would seem probable that he was from the first a worshipper, in some sort, of the true God. . . . . The chapters before us exhibit him at the critical juncture when he stood, partly on the domain of Gentile magic, and partly upon that of true revealed religion and prophecy; and deliberately proposed to maintain his ground upon both " (I. 738).

We have ourselves no doubt that every fact in the Scripture, when properly investigated, can be as conclusively proved as this miracle with the donkey.

The Deluge.   In the account of the salvation of specimens of all animated beings from the flood in Noah's ark, one objection always taken is, how light could have been thrown throughout the huge fabric in its three stages by one window in the roof, of the dimension of a cubit, or about eighteen inches, as its utmost dimension anywhere. The difficulty is now removed very effectively. "The window may have been a window course." This admits of plurality, and what "may have been," should the pressure of the necessity require it, assuredly was. On this certainty our interpreters proceed to deal with the matter, and the necessity still pressing, they repeat the range of windows ascertained to have existed as often as required. Here again is the safety of the multiplication table, as in the genealogies. There might have been thirty such ranges, but three suffice, one for each stage, besides the sky-lights in the roof. "It is by no means clear," they point out, but without embarrassing themselves or us with the grounds of their suggestion, "that these windows were all in the roof or deck. They may have been in the gunwales, *i.e.*, in the higher part of the sides of the vessel, like the port-holes of a modern ship of war." Quite so, like our three-deckers, which have recently passed out of use. Then these windows were, it may be thought, glazed, and the deluge of rain pouring down justifies the conclusion that they were so. "It seems not impossible," our commentators modestly suggest, "that some transparent substance was used. This may easily have been known to the Antediluvians, who had made the progress in arts described ch. iv. 21, 22. Perhaps the invention was lost after the Deluge" (I. 68). What scope this gives for assuring ourselves that the saved beings were saved in comfort, and not subjected to the darkness, stifling, and stench imagined by Bishop Colenso and others, and which would properly have fallen to their lot only if Ahriman, and not Ormuzd, had shut them in. We have but to widen the glazed apertures, and to reduce their intervening partitions, to convert the line of battle ship into a crystal palace. Then if the glazing were a lost invention, there may have been other inventions also, equally lost afterwards, which were then in full use. There were of course funnels to carry off smoke, and ventilators to circulate air through every part of the vessel. There may have been means to inject water through the premises, or water in some way "laid on," and pumps worked, we will say by the elephant or rhinoceros power within, to eject it with all accumulating refuse. There may have been apparatus for dragging the ocean around, sweeping in the fishes and drowning animals for food, and the submerged vegetation for fuel, and for supplying the herbivorous tribes. There may have been means for curing and preserving the saved meat and herbs, so as to have a lasting stock, better effected even than managed by us in this day. Then we hear of "representative" men, our commentators evidently adverting to the names in the tenth of Genesis occurring after the time of Noah. Noah may have been one, and there may have been many Noahs, Shems, Hams, and Japhets, and therewith many arks—a whole flotilla in fact. Instead of rolling about in a dark prison-house, in gloomy solitude, the saved beings may have been multitudes, lodged in sparkling floating palaces, enjoying happy communion together by telegraphic or other means now unknown to us.

These are the facilities for understanding so far the otherwise unintelligible story with which our commentators supply us, and it would be foolish not to use them. Then as for the mass of water required to cover up mountains five miles in height, and the insuperable difficulty of gathering in to one centre animals of the arctic, torrid, and intermediate zones, including the minutest ephemeral insect tribes, and keeping them all alive for the space of a year, and then returning them, none the worse for the expedition, to their proper quarters of the globe, bridging over all intervening seas in so doing,—by an easy method our commentators keep clear of all such obstacles maliciously thrown in the way by objectors.

" The Deluge," they suggest, "is described as from the point of view of an eye-witness," rather than " from the point of view of the Omnipotent. . . . . In all probability we have in Genesis the very syllables in which the Patriarch Shem described to the ancestors of Abraham that which he himself had seen, and in which he had borne so great part."

This view, they assure us, would in no way interfere with " the divine authority of the narrative." The witness describes just what was presented to his own eyes ; and could he properly have done more ? We fancy him at one of the glazed windows of the ark, note-book in hand, jotting down the particulars. The locality may have been " the region round about Babylon, with few hills in sight, and those not of great

altitude." Having been on the spot, we can relieve
the narrative here entirely. There are no hills
in that locality. Some little variation of level is all
that would have to be provided for. The narrator
was, we presume, speaking under the exaggeration
of fear. We should have thought the record tampered
with, but that our commentators consider we have
his very syllables. The judgment, they observe, would
be complete, if carried out over the inhabited portion of the globe merely. And then they suggest a
difficulty, but only to remove it.

" If it be inquired why it pleased God to save man and
beast in a huge vessel, instead of leaving them a refuge on
high hills or in some other sanctuary, we perhaps inquire in
vain." (I. 75-78)

Perhaps we do. It must generally be in vain to
inquire for God's unrevealed reasons. This affords
a ready answer for every apparent incongruity and
enormity placed before us in the Scriptures.

We have other instances than the above of the Unscientific
inspired author writing down as what was, what only Science.
seemed to be, giving descriptions "from the point of
view of an eye-witness," rather than from that of
"the Omnipotent," the occurrence of which quite
supports our reverend commentators in their solution
of the narrative of the deluge. The coney and the
hare do not really chew the cud, as alleged in Lev.
xi. 5, and made, in fact, the ground of a divine ordinance for the Israelites. These animals " have not
the peculiar stomach of the true ruminants, which
is essential to the act of rumination." They have
merely a nibbling motion of the jaws, which, to the
uninstructed observer, might pass for rumination ; and
" scientific accuracy," we might say accuracy of any

sort, was not here called for (I. 546). In the same way the bat was ranked as a bird, there being no requirement at the hands of the inspiring author for "a scientific classification of animals" (I. 546, 550), leaving him and his instrument at liberty, therefore, to present us with an erroneous classification. We would rather have suspected the hand of the errand-boys here, if allowed the option.

Our commentators are little troubled by the double, and somewhat conflicting, accounts of the deluge traced out by Colenso and his party. This is probably because they see no difference between two and seven, in one place there being but two pairs of beasts to be saved, and in another seven pairs of such as were "clean beasts." They say, "In any case there is no inconsistency between this verse" (Gen. vii. 2) "and ch. vi. 20, 'two of every sort.'" The command for the seven was "but an amplification of the former injunction." (I. 69).

The Exodus. We arrive now at the Exodus, in respect of the characteristics of which Bishop Colenso especially, among objectors, has given himself, and we may add ourselves and others, such a vast amount of needless trouble. The miracles were of course really such ; for what would the Bible be without the miraculous ? Marvels are sown through it broadcast, up and down. Exclude them, and the sacred volume would become more denuded of spirit, more decidedly emasculated, than the play of Hamlet without Hamlet. But sometimes the divine being who operates in the Bible does not go more out of his way than he can help in effecting his purposes ; and therefore, and perhaps to prove to us that these miracles were wrought in Egypt, and not, for example, in England, or elsewhere, the plagues selected were just such as were "in general accordance with natural phenomena" in the land (I. 279).

Then there is the passage of the ransomed people through the wilderness. They were there for forty years. What they were about for the greater portion thereof—that is, for the thirty-eight years intervening between the first year and the last—it is hard to judge. God's "covenant" with the people, "though not cancelled, was in abeyance." It was simply this. God having undertaken to save them, brought them with a "high hand" out of Egypt. But he found cause to change his mind, and to kill them off. God, by the hand of Moses, selected twelve persons, we presume chosen for their competency and trust-worthiness, to enter the promised land, and, among other things, judge of the people who had there to be subdued, "whether they be strong or weak, few or many" (Num. xiii. 18); and the report of ten out of the twelve was that their own party would not be able to conquer them. For not believing, preferably, the other two, God resolved to break his word with them, or, as our commentators state it, put his covenant, or agreement, into abeyance, and make an end of them all. And this, though in the final results the ten men proved to have formed a right judgment to a considerable extent, for the Israelites never managed to triumph over all whom they were divinely commissioned to exterminate.

We have to apologise for thus interrupting the thread of our commentators' discourse, but we thought to explain about the covenant thrown into abeyance. This being so, they add, in regard to the thirty-eight years of detention which are in question, "a veil is

accordingly thrown by Moses over this dreary interval
during which the rebellious generation was wasting
away." So he says little or nothing of what then
passed, which certainly serves to sadden the marvellous triumph of the exodus. But during this lengthened
period we are happy to think that these poor people
were not suffering all those wants and miseries so
gratuitously imagined by Bishop Colenso, and, in fact,
commonly believed to have made up their lot. They
" had traffic in provisions with surrounding tribes,"
being, of course, well stocked with the bullion which
they had borrowed of the Egyptians. "Indeed, the
regular highway of the caravans from the East to
Egypt, and *vice versâ*, lay across the Desert of the
Wandering." They are thought to have caught "fish"
in "the gulf of Akabah," and are now ascertained to
have been in the midst of considerable "fertility,"
belonging to some "population" there possessed of
"wealth." We certainly had concluded that they were
kept from actual starvation simply with the heavenly
supplies, as it is written, "And he humbled thee, and
suffered thee to hunger, and fed thee with manna,
which thou knewest not, neither did thy fathers know;
that he might make thee know that man doth not live
by bread only, but by every word that proceedeth out
of the mouth of the Lord doth man live" (Deut. viii. 3),
a lesson that obviously would be interfered with had
they also at command *ad libitum* supplies from earthly
sources. But having, as our commentators show,
such abundant help from the people around them,
it has assuredly been very sly of Moses to suppress
all this in order to arouse our commiseration for
himself and his people, by making it appear that
they were habitually "led about" "in a desert

land, and in the waste howling wilderness," (Deut. xxxii. 10). "A land," as the inspired Jeremiah afterwards characterized it, "of deserts and pits, a land of drought, of the shadow of death, a land that no man passed through" (how very wrong of him to say this), "and where no man dwelt," (probably meaning in houses) Jer. ii. 6. But it clearly was not so. Not only were they able to live as others, but with "these natural resources, supplemented where needful by miraculous aid" (I. 720), they were better off than the "wealth"-possessing "populations" around them, as was befitting even for the rejected people of God. We should consider it confusing to be thus dealt with, never knowing when we were to look out for ourselves, or when to trust for showers of provisions from heaven; but this schooling answered in the case of the Israelites as they were ever under divine guidance.

Our commentators have given us a valuable chapter on Egyptian history in association with the people of God. We suppose the information was desirable, and has therefore been traced out, though, for our own parts, we have a sense we may say of the irreverent in looking for the corroboration of a divine work to human sources. Still, we are not prepared to deny, what many allege, that the Egyptians have been favoured with a climate peculiarly calculated to preserve their monumental remains, for the very purpose of illustrating, and even perhaps of defending, the Bible representations. We do not therefore absolutely turn away from this historic support. *[margin: Egyptian History.]*

Our commentators resort only to the latest Egyptologists, Mariette Bey, de Rougé, Chabas, presuming that we are already acquainted with the older ones, in fact, have used them up. Manetho gives thirty-one dynasties of Egyptian rulers from Menes to Darius. The question is, under what sovereigns the different events of Hebrew history, as connected with Egypt, occurred. That is, the visit of Abraham when the then king of Egypt lost his heart, and, we should say, his head also, to Abraham's elderly wife, Sarah; when Joseph became prime minister and the saviour of the country; and when the Israelites multiplied there, and finally took their departure for what they considered their own land, since known as Judea.

The name-
less kings of
Egypt.
We should have had an easier task in ascertaining the Egyptian kings to be associated with the Hebrews had the sacred historian given us their names. Of course they were known to him, but for some wise purpose he has withheld them, though, in other instances, he has not been so reserved. We hear thus of Amraphel, Arioch, Chedorlaomer, Tidal, Bera, Birsha, Shinab, Shemeber, all great kings of various places, with some of whom Abraham went to war and routed with his household followers. We have the name of another royal personage, Abimelech, who fell in love with Sarah when she was considerably more stricken in years than when she caught the eye of the king of Egypt. And we have even five-and-twenty dukes of Edom, and seven of their predecessors, dukes of Hori, all properly named. There must then have been some good reason for withholding from us the names of these Egyptian kings.

The
Pharaohs.
But we are not quite accurate here. They are each called Pharaoh, as if that was the name they severally bore. "Pharaoh king of Egypt" is always the method, as we should say, "George king of England." It comes to us as a name, though possibly not a name in full.

But no such name appears on any Egyptian record, which so far is unfortunate. Hitherto, our Egyptologists, in laudable desire to support, we will say, Egyptian history with the Bible, have imagined that Pharaoh was titular, and expressed "The sun-god," by which title they assured us all the kings of Egypt were known. But this has been now found, as our commentators point out, not to be the case. The older Egyptologists should not have made a guess, and certainly not a wrong one. Pharaoh, they said, is made up of the article Pa, and Ra, the name of the sun-god, but the introduction of the article appears to have been a mere invention. "It," (the word Ra), "had not the article prefixed, and could not therefore be pronounced Pa-Ra, or Pharaoh." "The king is always called Si Ra, son of Ra." "He was not likely to be called both son of Ra, and The Ra." The guess might have been said to be nearly right, but not quite so, but that now a true interpretation presents itself, dispensing with the god Ra altogether. "If the transcription Per-ao, or Phar-ao, can be relied upon," (we would rather have been spared the opening for a doubt,) "the proof of the identity with Pharaoh will be conclusive;" or, in other words, if the thing be there, there it is, which is just what we want. But there is some little difficulty with regard to this hieroglyph and its meaning. The leading character may stand for "Pi," or "Per," or "Pere." The first is not desirable, as it is without the "R" required for Pharaoh. In one quarter it is held to mean "the great house," which would do. Such a sentence as this is presented to us : "His majesty, the *sovereign*, full of life, health, and might." "Pharaoh alone would represent to a Hebrew the central group in the Egyptian formula ; "

by which we understand the Hebrew eye would be
attracted to "Pi," or "Per," or "Pere-ao," "the *sovereign*," which it certainly would be if set out, as here,
in italics, more especially if the Hebrew eye were one
like that which watched the Deluge, or the coney and
the hare nibbling.   Then the leading character may
be duplicated, presenting to us "Pere pere," which it
appears would be embarrassing.   But we need not be
cast down about the matter.   Mr Birch, a considerable
authority, actually thinks he has discovered quite
another set of hieroglyphics for Pharaoh, though our
commentators do not favour him, and many more such
may come to light.   Our commentators prefer "the
great house," which they render as "sovereign," giving
us, therefore, "sovereign king of Egypt," to whom
the inspired author points whenever he speaks of
"Pharaoh king of Egypt."   But we do wish in our
secret hearts that he had given us the names.   This
invaluable description appears in pp. 477-479.

So now we have to fix upon the required kings
without knowing their names.   It is a sort of riddle.
We consider our commentators to have been very successful always in solving it.

Our commentators do not agree in this endeavour
with "Brugsch and others," who have gone before
them.   This is but natural.   It is, in fact, always so;
and though we are far from wishing to shorten the days
of our friends, we hope they may not live long enough
to find others springing up to overthrow their views,
as they have done those of their predecessors.

Our friends, if we may be permitted so to designate
them, give us a very lucid tabular statement as a summary of their detailed representation of their views,
(I. 473-475).   We there see in one column the Egyp-

tian dynasties and kings we have to deal with ; in the
next, the characteristic transactions of their reigns ; in
the third, the views they, our commentators, hold ;
and in the last, those of Brugsch and others, which, if
they be wise, will speedily be abandoned by them.

Our friends are satisfied " that Abraham visited
Egypt in some reign between the middle of the
eleventh and the thirteenth century, and most probably under one of the earliest Pharaohs of the
twelfth " (I. 447). How certain it becomes that these
kings are all to be known as Pharaohs! The pre-
ference is given to the twelfth dynasty, which is
natural, as it stands between the other two. It is
like striking an average for the sake of greater certainty. Having arrived so far, they proceed to choose
their king, and out of the seven of this twelfth
dynasty they select the first Amenemha I., while
they remit the premiership of Joseph to Amenemha
III., also of the same dynasty (I. 451). The reason
for this, as given in the summary, is, that there was
" a period of great prosperity ; foreigners, especially
from Western Asia, received and promoted under
the early kings ; and under the later kings works
of extraordinary magnitude executed to secure the
irrigation of Egypt and to guard against the re-
currence of famine." This is decisive, but also elastic.
If we ourselves had had ancestors in those days,
which of course is not impossible, some of them at
this time, taking advantage of the prevailing tran-
quillity, may have made a tour up the Nile (but
without, we trust, any female member of the family,
of whatever age) ; or, encouraged by the liberal feeling shown to foreigners, have obtained commissions
in some Pharaoh's army. We cannot, however, pre-

Visits of Abraham and Joseph.

tend to bring our supposed ancestors so close to the period as the irrigation works bring Joseph. How strikingly these works present to us the seven years of famine in his days! We are surprised that Brugsch and others were not arrested by the verification. These wander away, seeming scarcely to know where to go for their applications, which are entirely wanting in the precision characterizing our men. Abraham and Joseph, according to them, may have been in Egypt any time between the 12th and the 19th dynasties. They might have been there, so far as these now exploded delineations go, together, or even not at all.

Bondage of the Israelites. Our interpreters proceed with wonderfully clear adaptations. The Pharaoh who knew not Joseph is not actually pointed out, nor is a negative to be established. But the beginning of the persecution of the Israelites might have been known, but is not, according to the summary. This is unfortunate, for the term of the "bondage" was a prophetic one. The persecution began at some time during the period from the 13th to the 18th dynasties, but became "systematic" in the reign of Aahmes I. or Amosis, the first king of the 18th dynasty. This is evident, because then "buildings of great extent were undertaken or completed with the aid of forced labourers or mercenaries." We are following the language of the summary. Here, then, we have at once absolutely indicated to us the presence of the Israelites and the treatment they sustained, for they were surely "forced labourers." The lady who saved Moses was Nefertari, the widow and successor of Amosis. The fact is established from the circumstance of her sex. But now the text and the summary seem somewhat to differ. The text says, "It is at once clear that the expressions used in Exodus to describe the Pharaoh by whom the Israelites were first persecuted, apply, in the fullest and most literal sense, to this sovereign (Amosis)" (I. 453). The point of resemblance traced is that he besieged Avaris and overthrew the Hyksos dynasty. It is not said here that the Hyksos were the Israelites. If they were, Manetho must have been wrong in representing them to have withdrawn at once from Egypt and founded Jerusalem ("Cory's Ancient Fragments," 173). But if not the Hyksos, the correspondence in other respects between the Israelites and Amosis, whatever this may be, (and our commentators may explain it in a future edition,) remains of course undisturbed. And here, in ascertaining that Amosis originated the persecution, and that it was not brought on gradually, when and by whom we know not, as represented in the summary, we have a fulfilment of the Scripture requisition to fix the act upon some one individual king. The terms are: "Now there arose up a new king over Egypt, which knew not Joseph," to whom the change of aspect towards the Israelites, and the setting task-masters over them, is ascribed, on which it is added, "And they built for Pharaoh treasure cities, Pithom and Raamses." The question is, who built Pithom and Raamses? if there were such cities; for he is the man we are in search of. It is not yet positively ascertained whether there were such places. Brugsch identifies Pa-chtum en Zaru with Pithom, while Chabas does the like by "the sanctuary of Tum" (note); and our friends give the closest indication they can of Raamses, and that it was Amosis who built it, by observing that he had a son named Rames

(I. 453, 454). Thus Amosis assuredly was the man. But then, as the persecution was, according to the Scripture, to endure exactly 400 years, and actually did endure 430 (Gen. xv. 13 ; Ex. xii. 40), is it possible that it was begun by Amosis, and put an end to by his wife or widow, Nefertari ? We, of course, reply yes, there being in the Bible, as well as in Pagan annals, instances of still [greater longevity. We see not, therefore, what induced our friends to ease off the beginning of the persecution in the Summary to some indefinite time before Amosis. Here, however, a little difficulty springs to view. This is always happening, to our infinite annoyance, though our friends, we suppose from conscious power of rectification, take it all coolly. The person who saved Moses was Pharaoh's daughter ; but Nefertari was Pharaoh's wife, and her parents, though doubtless royal, were of Ethiopia, not Egypt. Perhaps the telegraph boys have been at work here on the sacred text. The opposite party, led on by Brugsch, hold, as the summary makes clear, that while Amosis reigned the Israelites were in peaceable occupation of Goshen. And this with them goes on through the reign of Nefertari and eleven other reigns till we come to Rameses II., the third king of the succeeding or 19th dynasty. But here they club in the advent of Moses, and thus allow no time for the prophetic era of 400 years.

The two be-
ginnings of
creation.
The passage in question is curiously worded by our friends, "First beginning of the persecution of the Israelites." Was there then a second beginning ? We never heard of such a thing. But stay,—we remember now that there was this at the creation, and that several beginnings of the same thing, or

act, may consequently have been ingrained into our
planetary and terrestrial system. There was that
"beginning" when the sun was made. This was the
"beginning of all things," for surely the sun is all
things to us. And afterwards there was "the first
day," during which, and five following days, every
created object was called into being, God, at the close
of these, his working days of the week, inspecting
"every thing that he had made," and ascertaining
that it was all "very good." The sun was accordingly twice made, and hence perhaps his great size.
This two-fold creation, and thereby doubling of the
sun, looks like a discovery in science, made by our
commentators, perhaps unconsciously to themselves,
which may worthily be classed with those happy elu-
cidations of religious truth brought out by them in
the glazed port-holes of Noah's ark, and the elasticity
of the defective genealogies. Thus science and religion
progress together, advancing, in happy union, and
with resemblant strides, our progress in appreciating
the sacred record; and Pharaoh's journals, whenever
needed, come in with admirable precision, to give
independent historic value to the subject.

According to our friends, in the reign of Thotmes II., The Exodus.
the third ruler after Queen Nefertari, we have the
return of Moses, the Exodus, and the destruction of
Pharaoh. The annals of Egypt might have mentioned
the plagues and the finally awful catastrophe, but,
with great perversity, do not. We are enabled, however, to identify the period sufficiently, because this
reign was "prosperous," then represented a "blank,"
after which occurred a revolt as near to the scene as
Syria. And so in the next reign, that of Thotmes III.,
the chosen people were in the wilderness, and finally

in Palestine. This is well established by the corresponding circumstances in the Egyptian chronicles,
which are, that this king tried to regain his "ascendency
in Syria," and made "repeated incursions into Palestine, Phœnicia, Syria, and Mesopotamia." Brugsch
and his party place the entry into Palestine under
Joshua in the reign of Rameses III. of the 20th
Dynasty, that is, the eleventh ruler after Thotmes III.

The Egyp-
tian and He-
brew annals. Our friends, speaking by the author of this essay,
refer to the results of their adaptations of Hebrew to
Egyptian history with becoming modesty, but at the
same time warrantable satisfaction. They say:—

"It will be observed that, although the results of comparison of Egyptian and Hebrew annals are, and must be to
a great extent conjectural, inasmuch as no direct or distinct
notice of the events preceding the Exodus, or following the
occupation of Palestine by the Israelites is found on Egyptian
monuments, and no notice of Egyptian history occurs in the
books of Joshua, Judges, and Samuel, yet the conjectures
rest on data established beyond all contradiction" (I. 461).

By this we understand that though there was nothing,
they have seen everything. It is remarkable, certainly, that with two nations intimately associated
together for so many years, neither party has ever
indicated the presence of the other. Extreme hatred
must have been the cause, as there are things, and why
not people, which we hold in such abhorrence as not
to mention them. It is not the defect of annalists.
The Hebrew history is inspired, and there can be no
charge of incompleteness brought against it. Let us
see what sort of records the Egyptians kept.

"The collection of papyri in the British Museum," our
friends tell us, "of which the principal have been published

by the trustees, belong for the most part to this period. They were written either under Rameses II. or his immediate successors. They indicate a very considerable development of Egyptian literature. The writing is legible, and the composition includes a varied treatment of many distinct subjects, giving a tolerably complete idea of the social and political condition of the people, especially of those employed in the district adjoining Pa-Ramesson" (where the Israelites laboured as prisoners of war, I. 467). "It was quite natural to expect that, if the Israelites were settled in Goshen, or had been very lately expelled, when those documents were written, some notices of them would be found, some allusions at least to the events preceding the Exodus. Accordingly a writer, to whose industry and ingenuity we are indebted for some of the first attempts to decipher and explain the select papyri, believed, and for a time persuaded others, that he found abundance of such notices. He speaks of a true, original, and varied picture of many of the very actors in the Exodus, a Jannes mentioned five times, a Moses twice, a Balaam son of Zippor, and the sudden and mysterious death of a prince royal, &c. Since his work was written all the passages adduced by him have been carefully investigated, and every indication of the presence of the Israelites has disappeared" (I. 468, 469).

How very provoking! What a pity it is that all people have not the same eyes, for this discoverer saw a great deal, even when there was nothing. The void in the records is of course not brought forward by our commentators to prejudice their own views, but simply those of Brugsch, &c. Still, when the literature was so good, and so varied, one might have expected, when politics were in question, there would have been some notice taken of the daring invasion by the Hebrews of the Egyptian dependencies in Palestine, and of their defeats and presence at Pa-Ramesson, the chief attrac-

tion of the literature, where bodies of them were
actually, it is to be thought, at work compulsorily, as
prisoners of war.

Then there is an interesting incident during this
same reign of Rameses II. An officer of his cavalry
was sent on a mission to Syria, where he found the
Cheta (Hittites) in occupation, although recognising
the supremacy of Egypt. On his return, he crossed
the Jordan, passed through North Palestine to Me-
giddo, incurred great risks from the Shasous (independent tribes), and finally reached Joppa, where
the authority of Egypt prevailed and the journey
ended.

"No mention, we find, is made of Israelites in this
papyrus; none, indeed, was to be expected. The only designation for the inhabitants with whom the officer came into
contact was Shasous—that which the Egyptians gave to all
the nomad and pastoral tribes, probably including the Hebrews, who occupied the countries between their frontiers
and Syria" (I. 468).

How very sad!—the holy people in the holy land
and yet not to be distinguishably known!

These passages are cited by our authors to show
how wrong Brugsch and his party have been in maintaining that when these annals were written, the Israelites were in Egypt, or had just left it, the fact being
that they were in happy enjoyment of their divinely
conferred inheritance, barring the drawbacks of Philistines and others disputing it with them. The Egyptians must have been smitten with judicial blindness
not to have observed them there.

"However it may be accounted for," our commentators
remark, "it is certain that during the whole period between

Joshua and Rehoboam, the Israelites were not disturbed in the possession of the strongholds of Palestine although the Pharoahs " (Pi, Per, Pere, Pere pere-ao), " as we have just seen, retained an undisputed supremacy in Western Asia up to the time of Samuel and Saul " (I. 458).

Western Asia, be it noted, comprehending Syria and Mesopotamia, and therefore overlapping Palestine.

We have so far kept our course with our reverend friends through the more important parts of their present delineations. The journey has been full of instruction to us, and not altogether devoid of sources of rational entertainment. We feel now enabled, with opened eyes, to receive the divine word in the light in which it presents itself to their experienced and culti-vated understandings. The record can no more act as a stone of offence or stumbling-block to any one. It is lucid and truthful even in its mis-statements, and per-fect in its imperfections. We would liken it to the most resplendent of precious brilliants, were there one of magnitude sufficient worthily to represent it. In default, we adopt for the expression of our idea a product of human manufacture as equally appropriate, encouraged in our selection by that intimate associa-tion which exists, in matters of revealed imagery, between the human and the divine. The inspired word presents itself to our imaginative regards as an enormous prism. The sun-light of divine inspiration plays upon its facets, enriching them with bright and varied colouring. A little manipulation, a little shifting of position from side to side, just as effects may require to be altered or multiplied, draws out latent and unsuspected radiance. And the passage of

The parting of friends.

the light through stained glass, as when Ezra and his imitators have intervened, superadds, from foreign sources, a totally different hue. A borrowed light of human fabric may be substituted occasionally for the sun. Even a farthing rush-light will do something. Egypt and Chaldea, for example, may be placed under requisitions to build up the heaven-bestowed gift to Israel. Naughty boys may chip off pieces, or fasten on it extraneous substances of their own, but the true prismatic form and lustre nevertheless remain.

As we said, our journey with our reverend friends is now over, and, altering our costume, we have now to prosecute our path alone.

A PITIFUL EXCUSE.

My very first step is one that cannot be taken without an apology. I have to present my own views now of the subject in issue, how I best can, and I wish to do so, as my thoughts may lead me, without restraint. I have seen it said that there are matters of which *Luke 16:30-31* one may not be " persuaded," although assured thereof by "one risen from the dead." Discouraging as may be the experiment, still I wish to have it tried. Hitherto, in this investigation into the true origin of our antiquated record, guess work upon one side, and empty assertion on the other, is all that has been brought into the field to govern the inquiry. Let us see what may possibly be obtainable from those who certainly are in the position to afford us the most direct testimony.

MITRE COURT.—Before Lord Chief Justice Speechless-Speaker and a Special Jury.

B *v.* C.

THE PLAINTIFF APPEARS BY THE ARCH-SOLICITOR-GENERAL AND THIRTY-SIX OTHER COUNSEL OF THE MITRE BAR. THE DEFENDANT CONDUCTS THE DEFENCE IN PERSON.

The Arch-Solicitor-General—My Lord, our subject being a difficult one, replete with ramifications and perplexities, requiring history, logic, languages, science, and above all divinity, for its elucidation, and the Defendant proving to be one gifted with unsurpassable hardihood, it has been thought necessary to the interests of my client to bring to his cause the large and learned body of brethren by whom I am this day supported. With my client, the issue before us may be said to be a perilous one, rendering caution as well as capacity urgently desirable, and there being safety in a multitude of heads, we have put ours all together. Some are able to withstand the attacks of calumny without much damage, and most persons manage to

survive them. But my client is otherwise constituted.
If he suffers from assaults such as those of the Defendant, his very essence of vitality is imperilled; nay,
the injury insures his death (*sensation*). He is what
he says he is, or he is nothing. Defendant in effect says
he is not himself, and thus is nothing. In the present
instance, treachery is superadded to the violence.
For though no more than words are the weapons
used by the Defendant, in these words is death (*sensation*). The treachery is this: that Defendant is to
this moment a retainer of the Plaintiffs, pledged, and
even paid, to do the reverse of that which he has done.
The Plaintiff has, unfortunately, many ill wishers,
though himself beneficently inclined, except towards
his enemies, who are those whom no stretch of liberality can number among the elect and favoured few.
The Defendant, with others, had bound himself to
support the Plaintiff through thick and through thin.
He was to veil, and satisfactorily to overlay with im-
penetrable covering, his errors and weaknesses, if he
have any, and to magnify his virtues, such as can be
found. He was to think with him, see with him, act
with him, in everything. His own thoughts were not
to work in any way, but according to the Plaintiff's
thoughts. And having taken upon him this office,
and by some show of zeal risen to a high and very
confidential post, the Defendant has not scrupled to
act as if he were without a master, and least of all,
such a one as the Plaintiff. With the Plaintiff's
livery upon his shoulders, he has joined, encouraged,
and headed the persecutors (*great indignation*). The
assaults, my lord, as I have said, though in mere
words, are of deadly effect (*sensation*). The Plaintiff has not spared them. Remonstrances, warnings,

have been ineffectual, and others, also numbered among the retainers, encouraged by his audacity, have joined the hostile ranks. We feel that a supreme effort has to be made to rescue our much-revered client. Upon his existence, so exalted stands he in position, influence, and power, hangs the fate of multitudes—the fate, I might say, of the whole universe, including probably the stars, fixed and unfixed, and their inhabitants. But here I desire to speak with caution, the matter lying a little outside my instructions. Such being the nature of the injury aimed at all in the person of my client, and such the character of the transgressor, exemplary damages are, of course, required. We have, therefore, laid ours at the highest figure we could think of (*great applause*). Unworthy as we are, and unequal as we feel ourselves to so great a cause, my brethren and myself, not deterred by the perils of the position, are determined, sink or swim, to risk our professional reputation upon the coming issue. The labour being great, we have divided it, but not so our responsibility (*applause*). The combination of our names may effect something, if not our arguments. But these, too, we shall not spare (*hear, hear*). A cord, stronger than that with which we hope the Defendant may hang himself at the close of this trial (*applause*) binds us all together. We recognize the interests confided to us, and our own. In zeal we shall make up for whatever we may be wanting in matter. We have commanded attention hitherto for whatever we have said, here or in other places; and now we design to say everything that the, no doubt, willing ears we are addressing (*turning to the jury*) will be glad to receive. (*Rapturous applause.*)

My Lord, I will not further trespass upon your time.

It has been arranged among us that my brother, H. B. of Ely, shall open the case with the portion entrusted to him, after which we shall each follow with our several allotments; presenting thus, we trust, a happy combination of division in union.

(*The learned Counsel in succession address the Court in behalf of Plaintiff. The libel is found to consist of 1279 pages, in five volumes, which is equally divided among them, read, and commented on. Their witnesses are then examined by the Arch-Solicitor-General, and closely cross-questioned by the Defendant. The case turns upon the authorship of a certain book, and the document being a very ancient one, it is allowed to prove itself, custody and transmission being all that the witnesses speak to.*)

DEFENDANT.—My lord, it is with considerable reluctance, and with no disrespect to yourself or the gentlemen of the jury, that I express myself as somewhat dissatisfied with the ordeal to which I am now subjected. I am accused of having been a traitor to my post, and of having aimed at the destruction of a much honoured patron. This I stoutly deny. I have done nothing to be ashamed of. In the few words of mine that have been read and commented on before your lordship, I have done no more than to express opinions that may be taken for what they are worth. If erroneous, I shall be glad to have them set right, but this task, even with the opportunity afforded them, the learned gentlemen who stand opposed to me cannot be said to attempt. And these opinions are but my private ones, publicly expressed, according to a liberty allowed us in these days when the fire-test is not applied to those who have thoughts to give utterance to. The damages laid are expressed in milliards.

Be it so. As I never can command means to pay
them their sum troubles me little. But why I should
be punished at all for saying what I do believe, can
be justified only by those who are richly remunerated
themselves for saying what they do not believe. (*Order,
order.*) I have not called the authorship of the entire
book in question, as might be supposed from the
nature of this prosecution. I object merely to the
historical value of certain portions, as, for example,
when a certain person is found giving an account of
his own death. And from what has fallen from the
learned gentlemen on the other side, I perceive that
they are themselves quite abroad as to who indited or
put together certain parts. The gentlemen of the
jury will doubtless bear this in mind when dealing
with the allegation of the disputed authorship. My
learned opponents have brought forward a host of
what they term evidence. I do not envy them the
possession of one particle of it. It has not the merit
of being even hearsay. The document in question
was to have been laid up by its author in a certain
chest. Ages afterwards this chest is examined, and it
is not there (*sensation*). The chest itself has disappeared, no one knows how, when, or where (*sensation*). One Hilkiah is said, after a lengthened interval,
to have found the record. I vainly endeavoured to
ascertain from the deponents how this document could
have been lost and so found, or how it was to be
identified with the original one. Nothing, moreover,
of an enduring sort came of this alleged discovery.
Another period elapses, and one Ezra, who I believe
to be the grandson of the aforesaid Hilkiah, comes
forward with a document, to which every one to whom
it was then communicated is allowed to have been an

utter stranger. Is this to be identified with the original record? I think the question of custody, my lord, is pretty effectually disposed of, even by my learned opponent's own witnesses. Then there is the transmission of the document that did come to hand after such flagrant disconnection with the alleged original document. Through how many hands has it not passed, my lord, and such hands! Persons, as I have been enabled to draw out from my opponent's witnesses, who have not hesitated to tamper with the text, transposing parts, cutting out others—long and important genealogies, for instance—and introducing their own crude information as belonging to the original record. Even errand boys entrusted with the message have, as I shall be prepared to show, thus operated. Nor is this all. The whole document, long after it had seen the light, has been overspread with floods of vowels, of which there was not one before. How words may be altered, when their syllables can thus be made anything of, I need not stop to describe. And then we have the passage of the document into foreign tongues, made too by those who were foreigners to the original tongue. Precious as this document is to us, at least as much of it as can be recognised as authentic, is there not an opening, my lord, for the expression on my part of those opinions for which I am now pursued with such vindictive damages?

My lord, I will now produce my witnesses. They will be found of a very different stamp to those on the other side. Mine are competent to speak direct to the point in issue, the question of the disputed authorship. I have had some difficulty in collecting them, for in a matter so antiquated they could be met with only in the other world.

The LORD CHIEF JUSTICE.—The other WHAT.

DEFENDANT.—THE OTHER WORLD, my lord (*great sensation*). It is a long way off, but I have spared no trouble in getting at them. Two are well known persons. The others are small boys whose names I have not been able to ascertain. I have, therefore, lettered those present according to the alphabet. (*Laughter, silence commanded.*)

MOSES appears. (*Intense and increasing excitement not to be repressed. One from the crowd at length steps forward and addresses the court.*)

AMICUS CURIÆ.—My lord, the examination of this personage, as if a common man, is more than we can bear. To question him is to shock the faith of ages. We object to have things thus sacred to us entered on in this manner, and our belief disturbed. We would rather subscribe and pay appellants' damages than that this should go on. (*Great applause, but some button up their pockets and leave the court.*)

The LORD CHIEF JUSTICE.—Sir, I have listened to you patiently in deference to the importance of the subject and the feeling of the people. But your interference, however natural, is not regular. It is for the counsel in the case to take the objection.

The ARCH-SOLICITOR-GENERAL rises and objects. (*An animated discussion ensues ; Defendant's voice drowned by the other thirty-seven voices.*)

MOSES.—Why, what's the matter? I'm a mere man, ain't I? (*Is told not to interrupt the proceedings.*)

DEFENDANT.—My lord, the other side frequently examine this witness, or one they say is he : and why may not I?

The LORD CHIEF JUSTICE (*after some considerable*

hesitation).—Well, let the examination proceed. (*The thirty-seven counsel for Plaintiff rise and make a solemn protest against the step.*)

The LORD CHIEF JUSTICE.—My brethren, this is not quite in rule. You should bow to the decision of the Court. (*The thirty-seven gentlemen rise together and bow profoundly.*)

MOSES, examined by Defendant.—Was an Egyptian priest; became a Dissenter; bore the name of Osarsiph.

The LORD CHIEF JUSTICE.—O-WHAT!

MOSES.—OSARSIPH, my lord. It is an Egyptian name. Changed it to Moyses, not Moses, for political reasons. Pentateuch? Who is that? Oh, a book. Did not write a word of it (*sensation*). Never plagued any one. Never heard of Pharaoh. There was no such king (*sensation*). Walk through the Red Sea? What do you mean? What, over the bottom of it dry shod? What arrant nonsense! Well, then, if you will have it, I never made such a passage. Was never on Mount Sinai. Don't know it (*sensation*). Never saw any divine being. Never spoke with one face to face. Certainly not. Did leave Egypt. Rebelled and headed a band of lepers. Sorry for it afterwards. Got no good by the move. We were defeated, and fled. Went to Palestine (*sensation*). Were not forty years on the way; what nonsense! Did not die in the desert.

Cross-examined by the ARCH-SOLICITOR-GENERAL. Was I a foundling? I was not. I came of honest parents, who took every care of me. What? Put into a basket and left by the Nile! and by my own mamma? You mean to insult me. Well, then, I was not. My mamma was incapable of such an act.

I a Hebrew! Don't know what you mean. I was an EGYPTIAN, I tell you. Nefertari—Nefertari? I knew no such person. I was educated at home, and not elsewhere. Pharaoh? No; there was no such king. Should think I *did* know the names of my kings. Don't you know yours? (*Is told not to question, but to answer.*) Oh, not exactly a name then! Well, what is it? A titular name. That means a name of some sort. Never heard such a name. All our kings bore it? Certainly not. *Pi, per, pere, pere pere-ao!* Whatever do you mean? There is no such word. Can I read Egyptian? Should think I can. Wasn't I a priest? Let me see the papyrus. Why, you have misread it. It is, *pooh, pooh, Oh!* It means—well, if you don't want to know, I won't tell you. Changed my name for an inheritance? No; I got one afterwards. Did not go by the Red Sea anyhow. That is not the way at all (*sensation*). Sinai? Know no such place. Called also Nissa? Yes, I know where that is. It was one of our holy places. One of our gods was born there. Which? Why, Osiris to be sure, our greatest god.

The LORD CHIEF JUSTICE. The greatest god! Explain yourself. There is but one.

MOSES.—I mean, my lord, that god who was partly man and partly god; who was put to a violent death; who rose again to life; who descended into hell, and has become the judge of the dead; who is in fact all in all to us.

The ARCH-SOLICITOR-GENERAL.—My lord, I submit that all this is irrelevant—mere fables, my lord. The witness is garrulous. (MOSES *looks at him fiercely.*)

The LORD CHIEF JUSTICE.—Well, well; proceed with the examination.

MOSES.—Well, as to Nissa, or Sinai, if you will have it, the birthplace of Osiris. (*Some one near appellant calls out, "Afterwards known as Bacchus."* *Silence commanded.*) Bacchus! Bacchus! who was he? (*Voice in crowd. " Why,* YOU *to be sure; you were Bacchus. Don't you see the connection with Sinai now?*)

The LORD CHIEF JUSTICE.—Who is that who dares to disturb the proceedings? Bring him up. (*Search made, but without results. The examination continued.*)

MOSES.—Well, I never was there, nor near it. Certainly not. Did I see no god? Certainly no god. I swear I never saw a god anywhere. *I* wear a veil because my face shone too much! Whatever do you mean? You are amusing yourself with me, Sir. Should I be surprised if my brother Aaron said he saw me descending from the mount? I should: I had no brother (*sensation*). *I* make him a priest, and not remain one myself? You are joking, surely! Would *you* act so? (*Is told not to ask impertinent questions.*)

The ARCH-SOLICITOR-GENERAL.—Come now, tell us something about the two tables. You remember, surely.

MOSES.—The WHAT?

The ARCH-SOLICITOR-GENERAL.—The two tables of stone.

MOSES.—We never used stone tables. Our tables were of—

The ARCH-SOLICITOR-GENERAL (*interrupting*).— Come, come, sir, no trifling. You know very well what I mean. I am asking you about the tables of stone written upon with the finger of God.

MOSES—What god?

The ARCH-SOLICITOR-GENERAL.—Why, your god, every body's god.

MOSES.—What, Osiris?

The ARCH-SOLICITOR-GENERAL. — No, sir; JE-HOVAH.

MOSES.—Well, you do change the names so, I can't follow you. Tables written upon with the finger of God! Surely it is *you* who are trifling with *me*. What, fingers on stone, and not on papyrus ! And why on stone? Oh, for the sake of durability was it? And did I see it? What nonsense! I did not; nor could any one ever have seen such a thing. *My* god Osiris commit such a folly ! and in *my* presence !!

The ARCH-SOLICITOR-GENERAL.—I did not say Osiris, sir. Why, here are your very words: "And the tables were the work of God, and the writing was the writing of God, graven upon tables."

MOSES.—*I* write that ? When, pray ? Where ? In my book ? I tell you I never wrote a book. Not such a fool. You are trying to catch me.

DEFENDANT—(*much excited*)—My lord, this is all drawn out to convey a covert insult to me through my ignorant witness, as it is well known I write books. (*The* ARCH-SOLICITOR-GENERAL *and the other thirty-six learned gentlemen rise and say mildly:* "*Why, my lord, we are writing a book, all together.*" *Suppressed tittering. Silence called. The examination is continued*).

The ARCH-SOLICITOR-GENERAL.—Now recollect yourself; these tables contained laws divinely imparted to you, and which you adopted for your people.

MOSES.—What people ?

The ARCH-SOLICITOR-GENERAL. — Why, *your* people—the Hebrews, to be sure.

MOSES.—Hebrews! *My* people! Never heard of them. Don't know the name even (*sensation*). Yes, none in Egypt that I ever saw or heard of. Abraham? No.—Joseph? No.—Jacob? No; I tell you, no. I don't know who you mean. And what were these precious laws?

The ARCH-SOLICITOR-GENERAL.—That you were to prefer your god to all other gods, and were not to kill, steal, covet, &c.

MOSES.—And do you mean to say that these common precepts were for the first time made known to me by the god you name? To me, who had the sacred books of Thoth, divinely given thousands of years before my time! You must be mad.

The ARCH-SOLICITOR-GENERAL—I am not, sir. I know quite well what I am about. It is *you* who were mad with passion when you threw these holy stones to the ground and dashed them to pieces.

MOSES.—What *I, I, I?*

The ARCH-SOLICITOR-GENERAL—Yes, sir, YOU. It was when you saw your people worshiping a golden calf, which you managed, somehow, to burn in the fire, to grind to powder, and mixing it in water to force down your people's throats.

MOSES (*in amazement*).—Down how many throats?

The ARCH-SOLICITOR-GENERAL.—Why, down the throats of the multitude with you, who numbered some two or three millions. After which you had three thousand of them killed off by the priests.

MOSES (*with solemnity*).—My lord, do you permit this? Have you understood the accusations made against me? I, a priest, to defy my god,—to dash his written stones to pieces,—to destroy the sacred effigy of Apis,—to murder his worshipers! My

E

lord, can you not protect me against these wanton and repeated insults?

The LORD CHIEF JUSTICE.—You appear, sir, to be ignorant of the course of justice in this land. Your feelings have nothing to do with the matter in issue. You have to speak to the facts simply put before you. Did you, or did you not, do as is alleged?

MOSES.—My lord, I scorn and defy you and your course of justice. You ought to be ashamed of yourselves for calling me up from my quiet resting-place to degrade and defame me thus.

The ARCH-SOLICITOR-GENERAL.—My lord, this is a peculiar case. The witness is evidently of an irascible temper, and the whole character of our proceedings is foreign to him. Defendant has called him forward, from where I know not, but evidently from some place far removed from our sphere. His evidence is highly important to us, could we get it. I humbly therefore pray your lordship will overlook his error and not commit him, as I see you are about to do, but allow the examination to proceed.

The LORD CHIEF JUSTICE.—Well, well. Make the best of it you can.

The ARCH-SOLICITOR-GENERAL.—Let me call your attention to these tables. You placed them by divine command in the sacred ark.

MOSES.—What, the broken pieces?

The ARCH-SOLICITOR-GENERAL.—No sir. Fresh stones, again inscribed by the finger of god, which were provided you. You know very well what I mean.

MOSES.—What (*sneeringly*), *more* durable ones I suppose than those I managed to break?

The ARCH-SOLICITOR-GENERAL.—Durable? Of

course they were, most durable, and laid up in the sacred repository I have mentioned.

MOSES.—Well then produce them. Let me see them. (*Dead silence.*) *Produce—produce* them I say (*stamping on the ground.*) This is all a sham, meant to insult me with.

The LORD CHIEF JUSTICE.—Leave the court, sir, this instant. (*Moses shakes his fist and vanishes with a terrific scowl. Intense agitation.*)

EZRA, examined by Defendant.—Pentateuch! Pentateuch! What is that? It sounds like Greek. Do I know Greek? A smattering. Have I met with Greeks? Often. Oh, its a book, is it? Don't know it. (*The Hebrew version is read to him.*) Well, its something like my mother tongue, but not exactly. Language changed? Yes, a good deal, especially as to the vowels. Do I know such a book? Well, I seem to know it. How much do I seem to know it? Why, more than a little. How much more than a little? Well, more than you do. (*Is rebuked for impertinence.*) Did I write it? I did (*sensation*). Did so with help. It was *not* all pure invention. Certainly not all *my* invention. Had some old documents to go by. What did I mean by seeking a consort for Adam among the brute beasts, and then bringing in Eve as an afterthought? Well, I cannot exactly tell you. We had, you know, but a low opinion of the other sex. How could Adam, in describing the matrimonial state, turn to speak of its involving separation from father and mother? Did I mean to imply he was conscious of having had human parents? Oh, no, no. That was not the form of the narrative at all. You must not be too particular. Who was Cain's wife? Who was Enoch's? Was it incest with sisters? Who were the people Cain feared would fall in with him and kill him? With what implements did Cain build his city, in the year 128 at latest? Who were its inhabitants when he had at the time but his son Enoch?—Well, well, well, you are too sharp by half. I hadn't *you* by me, you see, or I should not have tripped so. Cannot say where my ancient documents came from. Had also traditions. Got them from my neighbours—Greeks, Chaldeans, Persians, and Egyptians. Copied their rites freely, and some of their laws. Thought them good? Well, some of them—useful for the time at all events. Knew none better. Copied also their statuary and pictorial illustrations. These were very good. Thought them worthy of the celestial regions. Said in fact the originals were there. Did not feel that I was doing wrong. Did it from a good motive. Did it all in the name of Jehovah. Who was Jehovah? Surely you must know that. Said, in fact, that all I wrote came from Jehovah. Did so for the sake of my fellow-countrymen. We had all been in slavery in Babylon. Drew a good deal from that source naturally. We were much depressed. Sought to encourage and lift up my people. Persuaded them that Jehovah was with them. No harm in that; it was truth. Said that Jehovah had chosen them out of the whole world as his special favourites; that he had wrought wonders for them; and would work more. Drew a picture of their imputed founder, Abraham. Considered to be a fine portraiture of an old patriarch of those days. What about kings falling in love with Sarah when of a considerable age? How inquisitive you are! Well, that was a little thoughtless certainly, but it could not well be helped. Had to keep up her age to show

up a special and marvellous offspring, in whom to
centre all the divine promises. This actually afterwards, I understand, created the idea of the Messiah.
You see how important this was. His design to
sacrifice his own son out of keeping with the divine
character? It was not. I adopted prevailing ideas
quite suitable to human conceptions. Is it not a
worthy feeling to be ready to offer up one's only-
begotten son at the shrine of the deity? I, therefore,
most warrantably, said that Jehovah himself inspired
the thought. The designed sacrifice was no doubt a
grand idea. Vicarious suffering was our rule of justice
in sacrifice everywhere; but as the son had to be
saved to propagate the nation, I substituted for him a
ram. Jacob gaining his ends by a fraud? You use
harsh language. The ends had to be gained somehow.
Favoritism? No; it was election I had to exhibit.
Jacob elected and loved, though a transgressor? What
consolation I provided there for all my people! They
were transgressors in many ways, and perhaps most
of all in this, that they had a faculty for appropriation.
I bring this out later in my narrative in "the spoiling
of the Egyptians." How could I impute such things
to Jehovah—slaughterings, provision for concubinage,
and for slavery? You do not grasp the design of the
work. I had to build up my people, to give them a
solid central rallying-point. Promiscuous idolatries
unsettle the mind, introducing wavering and fastidious-
ness. I centred my people upon Jehovah; and to
attract and fix them there, had to make Jehovah
suitable to them. There, you have my whole secret.
I knew human nature well, and the nature of my own
people especially; and what chance had I of success
if I had warred against their propensities? Prophecies?

Yes. Miracles? Yes. What hope had I of imposing a divine word upon my people without these? Overdone? Not at all. Incredible? ridiculous? You little know those I had to deal with. They swallowed all greedily when it exalted Jehovah and themselves. How I managed about the prophecies? Well, some of the events had already come to pass. I was sure of these, and chanced the rest. Errors, do you say, as to some of the accomplished ones? Well, I am sorry to hear so. I did my best. Why did I parade facts as prophecies? You seem very ignorant. How else can you get unfulfilled prophecy to be accepted, but by showing some fulfilled. There you see; I am very open; I tell you everything. "Unto this day;" "Hebron;" "Dan;" "Gilgal;" "Canaanites then in the land;" "Kingly rule prevailing;"—what about all that? Oh, anachronisms were they? Well, they were mere oversights, and not many in so long a story. Moses recounting his own death and burial? You seem very gimlet-eyed. Could *you* have done better? Deuteronomy? What *do* you mean? Oh, that part. Did not write it (*sensation*). Am I sure? Well, almost. How nearly sure? Well, half—yes, more than half. Three-quarters? You are driving me too far. You want to catch me. Well, I *am* sure. Yes, certain. Yes, quite certain. How you do press one!

The LORD CHIEF JUSTICE, to Defendant.—You are occupying the time of the Court needlessly. The witness has already expressed certitude. (*Examination continued.*)

EZRA.—Well, *who* wrote it? How should I know? Was it before or after I wrote the other parts? Well, which you like. Must have been one or other? Of course it must. Happy to agree with you when I can.

Well, *I* must say, must I ? It was after. Long after ?
That depends upon what you call long. When was
it ? Do you mean *exactly* when ? Near about the
time I wrote. Was it before I wrote ? It was (*sensation*). How do I recollect ? Well, I shaped mine
differently. Purposely ? Yes, purposely. How you
do bother one! Well, it was chiefly in respect of
Tithes and Priests. He was too easy. I drew it all
together tighter. Why ? To please the priests, of
course. Did they become my friends ? Of course
they did. I was a priest myself. We all banded together. Priests always do. (*Voice in Court: "Not in
England." Silence commanded peremptorily.*) How
did I gain them over ? Provided them with feasts of
fat things to be sure. You seem very ignorant. The
people took it all in ? To be sure they did. They were
delightfully easy and superstitious. The thing took
immensely. It has taken here also, has it ? Delighted
to hear it. But I don't see how it is to help *you.*
My people took to it because I made them Jehovah's
favourites ; but what could that do for *you ?* (*Voice in
crowd: " The Christians are now the people of God,
and the Jews are rejected." GREAT APPLAUSE.*) Oh,
that is how it was managed, was it! Well, you
took a leaf out of my book. (*Great commotion, in the
midst of which witness is found to have disappeared.*)

The ARCH-SOLICITOR-GENERAL.—We waive our
rights, my lord. We have no wish to have the witness
called back for cross-examination. We have no re-
liance in these unsubstantial sort of people.

(*Enter small boy.*)

The LORD CHIEF JUSTICE.—Who is he ?

DEFENDANT.—My witness A., my lord.

.The LORD CHIEF JUSTICE.—Well, let us hear what
he can have to say to the matter.

A., examined by Defendant.—Know Ezra? No; my grandfather has spoken of him. An errand boy? No, I was nothing of that kind. Did I know any such? Of course I did. There was——

FOREMAN OF THE JURY.—My lord, are we expected to sit here while the Defendant is in search of evidence?

The LORD CHIEF JUSTICE.—Decidedly not.

DEFENDANT.—Then, my lord, I have no more to bring forward.

(*The parties severally reply and rejoin.*)

The LORD CHIEF JUSTICE.—Gentlemen of the jury, I thank you for the patient attention you have given this case. It is one without a parallel in some of its features. And it transcends in importance anything that has yet come before a human tribunal. The matter, however, lies in a nutshell, notwithstanding the volumes with which it has been overlaid. It is just this. Has the book that is in question come from its avowed author, or not? And are its contents, from its Alpha to its Omega, altogether reliable? With private opinions, or public, you have nothing whatever to do. You have to go entirely by the evidence laid before you. Which side do you believe, if either? Defendant was about to shower upon us a crowd of unknown witnesses, little boys, picked up by him promiscuously, who were to have been searched out by us to see what share they could possibly have had in the production of the book. The idea was on its face ridiculous, and you, Mr Foreman, by your sensible interposition, cut short this process at once. The Defendant has had thus to rely upon but two witnesses for his stupendous assertions. Are these persons themselves known as to their identity, and are their statements to be depended on? Do they impress you with their veracity or reliability? And does what they have been pleased to say amount to a justification of the alleged libel? These are the points you have to consider. The Plaintiff has a mass of evidence, stretching back beyond the memory of man, consisting of dignitaries, secular and ecclesiastical, men of learning and position, of every type and degree. Jews and Christians, hating each other cordially as they are entitled to do, here agree. Is that to be accounted for on any ground but the force of truth? It is for you to consider. On the other, or Defendant's side, we have two witnesses. I scarcely feel warranted in even terming them witnesses. If ghosts can be witnesses in respect of human affairs, do these two give us a ghost of evidence between them? What says Moses, or the object appearing as such? He seems to have been one Osarsiph if I caught the name rightly, an Egyptian, and not at all the person we were looking for. He could give us no information that I could gather of any kind. He knew nothing of this book—that is clear. Moreover, I am bound to say, he proved too irascible to be fairly and fully either questioned or understood. That, of course, is Defendant's misfortune; rather than his fault. Then there is the other witness. I feel I can safely leave him in your hands. Are you satisfied that his word is to be taken in anything? That he prevaricated at every turn was most apparent. It is for you to judge whether, nevertheless, there are residua of truth interspersed between what was of an opposite character in his utterances, such as serve to overthrow the whole weight of the testimony offered on the other side. The Plaintiff's Counsel allow that this witness had something to do with the matter of the book. The question is, how much? Whether to an extent to have

[handwritten margin notes: "Quick Tempered, Easily Provoked" and "To avoid Giving A Direct OR honest answer"]

warranted what Defendant has said of this book or not? That is a point you will weigh carefully. With these observations, I leave the case in your hands.

(The jury, without retiring, exchange a few words together.)

The LORD CHIEF JUSTICE.—Are you all agreed?

FOREMAN.—We are, my lord. We find for Plaintiff, with damages as laid. (*Great applause.*) In fact, my lord, we scarcely think these damages meet the requirements of the case, and we wish to double them. (*Immense cheering.*)

The LORD CHIEF JUSTICE.—I quite agree with you, and wish it were in my power to act upon your recommendation. But it is not. I can award no more than has been asked for.

The ARCH-SOLICITOR-GENERAL.—We are ready, my lord, to amend our request in any way you may allow. We are prepared to demand double, or even more.

The LORD CHIEF JUSTICE.—It is an unusual request, and I must take time to consider. In the meanwhile take the judgment given.

ASSOCIATE.—And the costs, my lord?

The LORD CHIEF JUSTICE.—Yes, yes, the costs go with the judgment, of course.

KEY TO THE TRIAL SCENE.

The Court, and the cause before it, are purely imaginary. The subject matter of the trial and the dramatis personæ can require no explanation. The tenor of the opening address by the Arch-Solicitor-General will also be self-evident. It describes, among other matters, the bondage of conscience under which the clergy unhappily lie. The Defendant's speech embraces the arguments connected with the custody and transmission of the Bible, its acknowledged inter-polations, the operation over it of the Masoretic vowel points, the errors of transcription and of translation, all of which are urged upon Bibliolaters, but mostly without effect. The criticisms, throughout, are those to which my own judgment has led me.

In treating this argument under its present form, I have endeavoured to give the scene that reality it would exhibit could such an ordeal as I picture be actually gone through. If what is ludicrous presents itself in my developments, this arises more from the nature of the matter in hand than from any effort of my own to place it in a light to excite mirth. My ultimate aim in my delineations is most serious. When we wish to expose that which is evil, we do so by stripping it of all pleasant disguises, that sin may appear in its proper aspect "as exceeding sinful." And when what is replete with absurdity, and manifestly incredible, comes before us, we take the same method. We peel off the veil of words and show things as they really are. The cause that I am labouring in, though easy of advocacy because guarded on every side by the safe defences of truth, and sure though it be of the ultimate triumph to which it is steadily advancing, at present,. in its infant stage, is retarded by that mountain of prejudice which refuses to give it a hearing. None of us therefore can afford to forego any usable advantage which the subject matter may give us, however loth we may be, in dealing with it, to wound the feelings of those still within the mists of darkness by which most of us were ourselves once environed. My liberties have therefore not been taken in wantonness, but with the view of making good my position and advancing my purposes.

I will now proceed with such explanations as may possibly be called for.

The bias of all concerned in this trial,—the judge, the jury, and the audience,—will be apparent. The pressure of orthodoxy, the defence of what is viewed as a divine position, effectually enslave the understanding and warp the judgment. The reluctance to have the Bible, as being a book from God, subjected to the examination and tests that may be applied to every other work, is represented by the commotion arising when Moses is brought forward for examination, and by the solemn protest of the professional gentry against the step when decided on.

Moses is the well-known Osarsiph of Manetho. The record has been preserved by Josephus, and will be found in "Cory's Ancient Fragments." I have discussed it, with all the needful bearings of the exodus, in my work, "The Bible; is it the Word of God?". The features of the history of Osiris, as adverted to by my Moses, appear in every work entering into the details of Egyptian mythology. They are succinctly set forth in Samuel Sharpe's admirable little treatise. He thus describes the connection with the Mosaic record.

"Of all the gods, Osiris alone had a place of birth and a place of burial. His birthplace was Mount Sinai, called by the Egyptians Mount Nissa. Hence was derived the god's Greek name, Dio-nysus, which is the same as the Hebrew Jehovah-nissi. This name Moses gave to the Almighty when he set up an altar to Him at the foot of the holy mountain, a spot sacred alike with Jews and Egyptians. See Exodus xvii. 15." (*Egyp. Myth.*, 10, 11.)

Dionysus is a name of Bacchus. The association of Moses with this divinity, is thus represented by Godfrey Higgins, drawing from Wood Gandell's translation of Abbé Bazin.

"In Bacchus we evidently have Moses. Herodotus says he was an Egyptian, brought up in Arabia Felix. The Orphic verses relate that he was preserved from the waters, in a little box or chest; that he was called Misem in commemoration of this event; that he was instructed in all the secrets of the gods, and that he had a rod, which he changed into a serpent at his pleasure; that he passed through the Red sea dry-shod, as Hercules subsequently did, in his goblet, through the straits of Abila and Calpe; and that when he went into India, he and his army enjoyed the light of the sun during the night: moreover, it is said, that he touched with his magic rod the waters of the great rivers Orontes and Hydaspes, upon which those waters flowed back and left him a free passage. It is even said that he arrested the course of the sun and moon. He wrote his laws on two tables of stone. He was anciently represented with horns or rays on his head" (*Anacalypsis*, II. 19).

Dr Adam Clarke, in his commentary on Exod. iv. 17, gives the like particulars.

"Cicero reckons five Bacchuses, one of which, according to Orpheus, was born of the river Nile, but according to the common opinion, he was born on the banks of that river. Bacchus is expressly said to have been *exposed* on the river Nile. Hence he is called *Nilus*, both by Diodorus and by Macrobius, and in the hymns of Orpheus he is named *Myses*, because he was drawn out of the water. He is represented by the poets as being *very beautiful*, and an illustrious warrior; they report him to have *overrun all Arabia* with *a numerous army*, both of men and women. He is also said to have been an eminent *lawgiver*, and to have written his laws on *two tables*. He always carried in his horn the thyrsus, a *rod* wreathed with *serpents*, and by *which* he is reported to have wrought many *miracles*."

The identity, it will be observed, is complete. The account by Higgins also includes Joshua's great miracles of effecting a dry passage over the fordable little river Jordan, and arresting daylight, by making, as the scripture will have it, both the moon and the sun to "stand still."

Moses is straight-forward and impulsive. He has had nothing to disguise. It is otherwise with Ezra. He is conscious of having played a double part, and gives his evidence with reluctance and prevarication. The statements driven out of him exhibit the prominent results of modern criticism in exposing the composite character of the record, its incongruities and anachronisms. The witness allows contact with other nations, the Greeks inclusive; the use of ancient, but now unknown documents; traditionary lore; and resort to pagan sources for rites and imagery. He acknowledges, what it is obvious was the case, that the Hebrews are represented to be the special objects of the divine favour, visited by his exclusive presence, upheld by his associated support, in order to encourage them after a time of ruin, and consolidate them as a nation; and has to admit that the elements of miracles and prophecies have been introduced in order to sustain these pretensions.

It is of great importance, in judging of the Hebrew record, to form a true estimate of the god Jehovah whom it enfolds. To this important subject I have devoted a separate section. If the conclusion I there come to may be accepted, it will, as a minor consequence, warrant the light in which I have ventured to place the salient historic details of the Pentateuch in my examination of Ezra.

In Ezra's deposition, the history of Abraham is referred to as drawn ideally. Drummond and Dupuis consider him a mythological character. Hyde and Higgins associate him with Brahma and Zoroaster. Inman and others criticise the facts of his history as untrue. Nor will they bear any proper examination.

Terah, the father of Abraham, is said to have been 70 years of age when he was born (Gen. xi. 26), and Terah lived to be 205 (ver. 32). Abraham, according to this, was 135 years old when his father died. And yet, we learn, that on leaving Haran, after his father's death, he was but 75 (Gen. xii. 4).

Abraham's great merit was his quitting his own country at the call of God to become a stranger and a pilgrim in another land. The apostle has it (most unwarrantably) that "he went out, not knowing whither he went" (Heb. xi. 8). This led to Jehovah adopting him to form of him a great nation in whom should centre all the promises. And if there was to be blessing to any other of the "families of the earth," it was to be through this elected stock (Gen. xii. 3). The movement, therefore, was a most important one; but what are its given circumstances? The family were of Ur of the Chaldees, and the appointed place of the pilgrimage was Canaan. But it appears that it was Terah, the idolatrous (Josh. xxiv. 2) father of Abraham, and not Abraham himself, who projected and actually commenced the movement. "And Terah took Abram his son, and Lot the son of Haran his son's son, and Sarai his daughter-in-law, his son Abram's wife; and they went forth with them from Ur of the Chaldees, to go into the land of Canaan; and they came unto Haran, and dwelt there" (Gen. xi. 31). The idolater, of course, knew what he was about, and went to better himself; and the scripture, than which there is never a better witness against itself than its own unguarded statements, negatives the whole fiction of the spiritual call of the founder of the divinely elected Hebrew commonwealth.

Bishop Colenso (IV. 282) gives a table showing how the patriarchs stood as to births and deaths occurring after the flood. Noah survived that event 350 years (Gen. ix. 28). In that interval Abraham was born, and he was of mature age when all his progenitors from Noah to Terah, ten in number, were still alive. For example he was 58 years old when Noah died. Three of them, Shem, Salah, and Eber, survived him,—Shem by 35 years. Yet not one of these, (excluding the father Terah,) is met with, or adverted to, in this veracious history. Taking the accounts of the flood and of Abraham to be true, Canaan and Egypt must have been occupied by Abraham's known ancestors and kindred, but all these are entire strangers to him.

We thus have Abraham located in Canaan, the region appointed to him by his father Terah. There he has habitual contact with the existing inhabitants. Especially we have an account of his bargaining for a place of burial with the children of Heth. He comes into contact with Melchizedec the king of Salem, with the kings of Sodom and of Gerar, and even with the king of Egypt, whose territories he visits.˙ But it never occurs to the unconscious historian that a Chaldee could not have held converse with any one of these tribes without an interpreter.

Then we have the ludicrous stories of kings falling in love with the pilgrim's wife, the king of Egypt when she was 65, and Abimelech, the king of Gerar, when she had reached the maturer age of 90. And the latter story is repeated again, as an occurrence taking place a hundred years later as between apparently the same Abimelech and the wife of Isaac. Sarah, it is to be observed, was at once sister and wife to Abraham, as was Isis to Osiris (*Sharpe's Egyp. Myth.*, 9, 10). Ceres, who was the Egyptian Isis, in like manner held this double position towards Jupiter, both having Saturn for their father (*Inman's Ancient Faiths*, I. 193, *note ; Lempriere*). The mythologies here unite.

It is considered to have been a marvel, lying beyond the range of all past experience, that Abraham and Sarah, at the respective ages of 100 and 90, should have had a son. "Therefore sprang there," observes the apostle, "even of one, and him as good as dead, so many as the stars of the sky in multitude." The narrative certainly in some way requires reconstruction when we find, according to the accepted chronology, that forty-four years later Abraham took to himself a second wife, who bore him six sons (Gen. xxv, 1, 2), at the birth of the last of whom his age must have stood at fifty years beyond the apostle's age of

Hebrews 11:12

F

marvel. And assuredly both the historian and the apostolic commentator quite overlooked what had been said as to the ages and the progenies of the earlier patriarchs. At this very time of the birth of Isaac, Bishop Colenso (IV. 283) points out that there were actually living, six who had attained the ages of 580, 390, 355, 325, 229, and 170, respectively, one of whom, namely Shem, had his first child when at the age of 100, after which he lived "five hundred years" more, "and begat sons and daughters" (Gen. xi. 10, 11). Consistency, fortunately, is hard to maintain in dealing out fiction.

We furthermore have Abraham, when over the age of 80, turning out with 318 armed domestic followers and overtaking four victorious kings who had just won a great battle with five other monarchs, and defeating and pursuing them over a mountainous region, and to a distance of 160 miles, to the neighbourhood of Damascus, slaughtering them (Heb. vii. 1), and wrenching from their hands his nephew Lot and all his pillaged goods captured at their taking of Sodom.

The sole remaining event to be noticed in this remarkable history, is the meeting with Melchizedec. He is described as "priest of the most high God, possessor of heaven and earth." Was this Jehovah who is described to us only as the god of Abraham, and ruling in Canaan? And if Jehovah, how did he pass over this sainted personage to centre all his blessings in the son of the idolatrous Terah? The apostle intensifies the fabulous character of the incident by describing Melchizedec as without human parentage, without "beginning of days or end of life," and "made like unto the Son of God," with a never-ending priesthood.

Hebrews 7:3

I have now but to explain Ezra's testimony as to Deuteronomy. All criticism distinguishes between this and the prior sections of the Pentateuch, nor have our commentators been able to do otherwise than to allow the distinction. But opinions differ as to how to account for the book, whether to ascribe to it an earlier or a later origin than that of its associated Exodus, Leviticus, and Numbers. This conflict I point to in making Ezra, in his prevarications, say at first that Deuteronomy followed, and then finally that it preceded the others; and I adopt the latter as the true solution in view of the most able examination of the subject given by Dr Kalisch in his commentary on Leviticus.

THE HEBREW GOD.

The real aim of the Hebrew record, there can be little doubt, was, through the powerful agency of a theocracy, to secure national stability and importance. We have possessed ourselves of the record, conceiving that it reveals to us the true God by means without which our knowledge of him, it is supposed, must have remained imperfect and erroneous. It is a matter, therefore, of consequence to us to understand the sources from whence the Hebrews derived their deity, how he is depicted as standing nationally for them, and how they served each other, the god and the people.

This divinity is proclaimed as being Jehovah. Was he, though special to the Jews, one whom we, nevertheless, may adopt as the one true and universal God?

"Jehovah," our commentators allow, "is as clearly a proper name as Jupiter or Vishnu. *Elohim* and *Jehovah* are therefore as distinguishable as *Deus* and *Jupiter*" (I. 24). "It is clear," justly observes Dr Inman, "that there is no necessity for nomenclature in heaven, unless more than one Being exist there. To assign, therefore, a name to the Creator, involves the idea that there are others besides Him" (*Ancient Faiths*, I. 620). And this writer indicates, whatever credit may be allowed to the Jews for monotheism among themselves, that their god stood in rivalry with other gods. The passages cited for the purpose are the following:—

" Who is like unto thee, O Lord (*Jehovah*), amongst
the gods?" (*Elohim*)—Exod. xv. 11.

" Now I know that the Lord (*Jehovah*) is greater
than all gods" (*Elohim*)—Exod. xviii. 11.

" Among the gods (*Elohim*) there is none like unto
thee, O Lord (*Adonai*)—Ps. lxxxvi. 8.

" For the Lord (*El*) is a great god (*Jehovah*), and
a great king above all gods" (*Elohim*)—Ps. xcv. 3.

" Worship him, all ye gods" (*Elohim*)—Ps. xcvii. 7.
" Our Lord (*Jehovah*) is above all gods" (*Elohim*)—
Ps. cxxxv. 5.

" Great is our God (*Eloah*) above all gods" (*Elohim*)
—2 Chron. ii. 5.

" The Lord (*Jehovah*) will famish all the gods of
the earth" (*Elohim*)—Zeph. ii. 11.

He is thus depicted standing like Jove in supre-
macy over the other divinities—" God of gods," and
" Lord of lords," "a great God," and "a mighty" one
(Deut. x. 17).

We may understand now the contract which Jacob
made with this particular god. "And Jacob vowed
a vow, saying, *If* God will be with me, and will keep
me in this way that I go, and will give me bread to
eat, and raiment to put on, so that I come again to
my father's house in peace; THEN shall the Lord be
my God" (Gen. xxviii. 20, 21). We can understand
also the formula of the divine command written on
the Mosaic tables, "Thou shalt have no other gods
before me." The other gods were there indisputably,
but they were to prefer Jehovah. He was "a jealous
god;" that is, jealous of "strange gods" (Deut. xxxii.
16). "He is an holy God," observes Joshua, "He is
a jealous God." "If ye forsake the Lord (Jehovah),
and serve other gods, then he will turn and do you

hurt, and consume you" (xxiv. 19, 20). His people were to be very careful not to "forget the Lord their God," who had signalized his presence among them with such mighty wonders, and, leaving him, "walk after other gods" (Deut. viii. 19). With his rivals he had shown what he could do when he "executed judgment" "against all the gods of Egypt" (Exod. xii. 12).

Our translators, it will be observed, veil, as often as they can, the too prominent "Jehovah" in the mere titular designation "Lord." The whole ceremonial appliances of the Jewish dispensation were to keep the people true to this Jehovah. The distinction between him and the surrounding gods was so small that they were always tumbling out of one worship into the other. The act was considered one of infidelity; such as when the marriage vow is broken; the seducing objects who tempt to the breach being as real as the one entitled to the faithfulness. The figure so far, therefore, was perfect. It was the one great struggle with the nation, if we are to accept its histories, during the nine hundred years from Moses to Ezra, to keep clear of promiscuous idolatries; and then the conflict ceased. The temptation was no more incurred. The nation became sealed irrevocably to Jehovah. Is it not plain that the great work of Ezra, in composing for them their sacred record, in giving them substantially their beacons and their law, was the cause? To this solution all criticism in the matter tends; and the two witnesses—the one the chain of evidence of the absence of the written law till Ezra's promulgation of it, illustrated by the practice, through this time, of the forbidden idolatries, and the other the sudden, solid, and perfected reformation—prove the case with a weight of testimony not to be subverted.

We may now safely inquire who was this Hebrew god Jehovah? The people were a copying race. Did they get him from others? The scripture meets any such suggestion by assuring us that he himself revealed his name to Moses. "And God spake unto Moses, and said unto him, I am the Lord. And I appeared unto Abraham, unto Isaac, and unto Jacob, by the name of God Almighty, but by my name JEHOVAH was I not known to them" (Exod. vi. 2, 3). The announcement made, could our translators have been brought to put it before us plainly, was "I am JEHOVAH," a name hitherto retained, it is alleged, from the knowledge even of the patriarchs. And yet, points out Bishop Colenso :—

"It is put into the mouth of the patriarchs themselves, as Abraham, Gen. xiv. 22, Isaac, xxvi. 22, Jacob, xxviii. 16. Nay, according to the story, it was not only known to these, but to a multitude of others,—to Eve, iv. 1, and Lamech, v. 29, before the flood, and to Noah after it, ix. 26,—to Sarai, xvi. 2, Rebekah, xxvii. 7, Leah, xxix. 35, Rachel, xxx. 24.—to Laban also, xxiv. 31, and Bethuel, xxiv. 50, and Abraham's servant, xxiv. 27,—even to *heathens*, as Abimelech, the Philistine king of Gerar, his friend, and his chief captain, xxvi. 28. And, generally, we are told that, as early as the time of Enos, the son of Seth, 'then began men to call upon the name of Jehovah,' iv. 26, though the name was already known to Eve, according to the narrative, more than two centuries before" (II. 231).

Our translators have maintained their carefulness to keep out of view the somewhat inconvenient "Jehovah," and present us, throughout these passages, with "the Lord," as if that had been the term used. We see now that there are two accounts in the scripture of the introduction of this divine name to the attention of human worshipers, one arising in the time of Enos, or the third generation from Adam, and one in that of Moses. And we find that the two accounts, as is common in the scripture reduplications, contradict one another, and may be seen, by the record itself, to be both untrue. Our right consequently increases to look elsewhere for the origination of the name among the Hebrews, so as the better to satisfy ourselves of the sort of divinity adopted by them under it.

After connecting king David with Greeks, Italians, Philistines, Babylonians, and Assyrians, Dr Inman says :—

"Among the Greeks we find the word Ἰαώ, *iao*, which corresponds clearly to the *Ju* in JUPITER amongst the Italians, and the Ἰα in IACCUS. The name IAO is explained in many ancient passages to be the equivalent of Helios, Aides, Zeus, Dionysus, Adonis, Attys, Iaccus, and Bacchus" (*Ancient Faiths*, I. 611).

He then traces the name Jah, Ju, or Jao, in the composition of Phœnician, Syrian, Assyrian, and Babylonian appellatives, bringing before us also the Phœnician divinity *Yâho*, or the sun god Baal. And he finds JAH and JAYA sometimes appearing as *Jaga* among the Aryan Indians, as in the familiar *Jaga-nath*,—noticing here, to support himself, that "we have the testimony of Rawlinson" to a "Vedic or an Aryan influence on the early mythology of Babylon" (I. 612-615).

"Bacchus," says Godfrey Higgins,

"Was called ΕΥΟΙ. This is the ΙΕΥΩ, ΙΑΩ, ΙΑΟΥ, or Yahouh, the same as ΙΕ on the temple of the Delphian Apollo. Bacchus was also called a Bull, and a Son of

God. . . . In the ancient books of the Jews, we constantly find mention made of the God Jehovah, who ought to be called JAH, or JEUE. . . . Diodorus Siculus says, that Moses pretended to receive his laws from the God called IAΩ. This shows that the Greeks considered the name of the Jewish God to be, not Jehovah, but, as I have stated it, יהו *ieu*, or Jeo. Iηϊος is one of the names of Apollo."

Then comes a citation from Beausobre, who says:—

" One must allow that it is Jehovah, which the ancients have written and pronounced sometimes Jaho, sometimes Jevo, and sometimes Iaou. But it is necessary also to allow that Iao is one of the names that the Pagans give to the sun. . . . Jupiter, Pluto, the sun, and Bacchus, are the same."

He also cites Parkhurst as an authority not to be disputed, who says that :—

" יהוה *ieue*, was well known to the heathen, there can be no doubt,"

His authorities being Diodorus Siculus, Varro, St Augustine, &c., to the effect that,

" The Iao, Jehovah, or יהוה *ieue*, or יה *ie* of the Jews, was the Jove of the Latins and Etruscans. . . . . He allows that this יה *ie*, was the name of Apollo, over the door of the Temple of Delphi."

After this, the testimony of Maurice's History of Hindustan is adduced to the circumstance that the

" Devatas of India sing out in transport in honour of Cristna, the words JEYE! JEYE!"

On which Higgins remarks—

"Here we have the identical name Jehovah."

Again—

"The followers of Iao, יהוה *ieue*, constantly sung the *Hal-lelujah* in his praise. This they did in the temple of Solomon, in the temple of Delphi."

Then comes a citation from Schiller, to the effect that—

"None dare to enter the temple of Serapis, who did not bear on his forehead the name of Jao, J-ha-ho, a name almost equivalent in sound to that of the Hebrew Jehovah, and probably of identical import; and no name was uttered in Egypt with more reverence than this of Iao."

After this, Shuckford is referred to as observing,

"That it is said by Philo-Biblius in Eusebius, that the god of the Phœnicians was called Jevo or Jao."

This divinity Higgins naturally identifies with the Grecian Jove, supporting himself here with Maurice. Mr Higgins then sums up—

"It is thus proved by fair deduction and logical reasoning on unquestionable authority, that the God יהוה IEUE, Jehovah, יה JE, or Jah of the Jews, the God ᴚI, the Apollo of Delphos, the Deus, the Jupiter, Jovis, Jovispiter of the Latins, the god Mithra of the Persians, and all the gods of the Heathens, are identically the same person or being. . . . In short, that Jehovah was the sun" (*Anac.* I. 322-331).

His solemn annunciation of himself as the ☩ AM THAT I AM, said to have been made to Moses when he received from him his commission in Egypt (Exod. iii. 14), was the Nᴜᴋ Pᴜ Nᴜᴋ of the Egyptian sepulchral rolls (*Lesley's Man's Origin and Destiny*, 151).

We have accordingly before us the sun-god, that power of nature universally reverenced among the surrounding nations. He is the Osiris of Egypt, the Yâho or Baal of the Phœnicians, the Bacchus or Apollo

of the Greeks, the Jove or Jupiter of the Latins, the
Bel of Babylon, the Mithra or Mitra of the Bactrians
and Aryan Indians; and now, it becomes apparent to
us, the Jehovah of the Jews, enshrined and localized
among them, in less exhibitional form, in viewless
majesty, between the cherubic images in the adytum
of their sacred temple.

Let us study a little the subject of idolatry.
An idol is something other than god, taking the
place of god. He is commonly represented by an
image, but not necessarily so. Higgins, citing Shuckford, points out that Numa, the second king of Rome,
kept his people free of images for 170 years, recognising the deity as invisible. Plutarch declares that in
the previous times also they were without images
(*Anac.* I. 47). The Zoroastrians had none, nor had the
early Aryan Indians. That Jehovah was thus unre-
presented is no evidence that he was the true God.
The idol is ever limited in his field, being proper
only to those who imagine him. He is strictly local-
ised, and something that can be walked round and
have his measure taken. If Jove was to be consulted,
he was to be met with at Dodona ; if Apollo, at
Delphi ; and if Jehovah, at Jerusalem. Every surrounding god from Egypt to India had his favourite
haunt—some shrine, in some distinct region, where he
had his appointed seat. Jehovah's throne was in the
holiest of holies, in the national temple, on the ark,
between the cherubim—symbols, one and all, derived from Egyptian idol forms.
The imitation god, when put to proof, is always
found deficient in power, in knowledge, and in morality.
His standard, in fact, can but be that of the people

who have made him. Jehovah wished to destroy the
Canaanites, in order to instal in their room his chosen
people. But "as for the Jebusites, the inhabitants of
Jerusalem, the children of Judah *could not* drive them
out" (Josh. xv. 63). The very seat of the divinity
failed to evoke from him power sufficient to expel the
outcasts. Other tribes held their ground against him,
and prominently the Philistines to the end. He was
baffled even by the common equipments of war.
"And the Lord was with Judah; and he drave out
the inhabitants of the mountain, but *could not* drive
out the inhabitants of the valley; *because they had
chariots of iron*" (Jud. i. 19). So far as to power.
In respect of knowledge Jehovah was not aware that
the sun, and not the earth, was the centre of our
planetary system. He thought the sun to be gyrat-
ing round us, and that he could stop him in his course
when needed for the convenience of his people, without disturbing other processes of nature. He considered the earth to be a motionless flat disc, supported
on foundations of some kind (Ps. civ. 5; 1 Sam. ii. 8).
Had it been subjected to revolving, its "ends" (Ps.
cxxxv. 7) would have been rolled up. He was no
naturalist. The hare, with him, was a ruminant; the
ant, bearing her white larva to her hole, was looked
upon as a type of providence, storing her granary as we
do ours at harvest-time (Prov. vi. 8); the whale, passing
from the icy north, entered the Mediterranean; dis-
tended its gullet to proportions hitherto unattained,
swallowed a prophet, who survived the operation,
came out, and in the sacred pages has told us of his
adventure; the eagle, planting her nest in unobserved
heights, "fluttereth over her young, spreadeth abroad
her wings, taketh them, beareth them on her wings"

(Deut. xxxii. 11), as when the god himself rides
through the air upon the eagle wings of the ox-headed
cherub (2 Sam. xxii. 11). Limited as was his information of things present, he liberally launched out in
proclaiming, out of faculties not dispensed to man,
what was to be revealed only in futurity; but not one
single prophecy uttered by him has been accomplished.
Miracles, or subversions of natural laws, he indulged
in very freely, though the ejection of Jebusites and
Philistines was beyond him. And one of the most
notable of these rests on the highly trust-worthy impressions of Balaam's fancy. The others are, one
and all, equally ill supported. But he was jealous of
rivalry in this magic art, and therefore "suffered"
not "a witch to live" (Exod. xxii. 18). So far as to
scope of knowledge. His moral attributes are on a
level with those of his people. He had his partialities,
"as it is written, Jacob have I loved, but Esau have I
hated" (Rom. ix. 13). This, we learn (Rom. ix. 10-13),
was before their birth, as signalised when Jacob, against
all that is yet known of obstetric art (*Dr Inman's
Ancient Faiths*, I. 600), passed, without risk to himself
or his mother, into this world, having fast hold of his
brother's heel. The system of hardening some for
judgment, as Sihon, king of Heshbon, and notably
Pharaoh; and favouring others in spite of their crimes,
as for instance Jacob and David, was habitual to him.
He was apt, moreover, to "repent," to change his purposes, and then could be turned back again to them
by the interposition even of a human adviser. There
is a remarkable example given in Exod. xxxii. 9-14,
where Jehovah begged Moses to "let him alone," that
he might vent his "wrath," which had "waxed hot,"
upon his people, and destroy them, the inducement to

Moses being that the god would "make of him a great nation," in substitution for the others. Moses, with praiseworthy abstention, happily exercised influence sufficient to divert the god from his design. This is by no means a solitary instance of the kind. Jehovah was, in fact, habitually impulsive, committing himself to indiscreet pledges and outbursts of passion; but then, seeing his errors, had the candour to fall back from them (Judg. ii. 18; 1 Sam. ii. 30; xv. 11, 35; 2 Sam. xxiv. 16; Jer. xviii. 8, 10; xxvi. 3, 13, 19; xlii. 10; Jonah iii. 10). His sense of justice led him to visit children for the transgressions of their parents (Exod. xx. 5; xxxiv. 7; Jer. xxxii. 18). In this manner he required to be appeased by the murder of Saul's innocent sons and grandsons for an alleged transgression committed by that divinely chosen, but, as it proved, ill-selected monarch (2 Sam. xxi. 1-9). His legislation was naturally shaped to feed the propensities of the people who had devised him. They were a savage race. He told them to "destroy" their enemies "utterly" (Deut. vii. 2). Not even women and children were to be spared, whenever their god was able to give his people the mastery over them. "Have ye saved all the women alive?" shouted out, on one such occasion, the meekest of men. "Now, therefore," he added, "kill every male among the little ones, and kill every woman." But here, remembering another propensity of the people, the virgins, even among the children, they were told might be spared in order to be devoted to prostitution (Num. xxxi. 15-18; also Deut. xx. 14.) With this unwholesome reservation, the pitiless order was, "thou shalt save alive nothing that breatheth; but thou shalt utterly destroy them" (Deut. xx. 13-17); an injunction faithfully carried out whenever the divine power sufficed for the atrocious purpose, as recorded in Deut. ii. 30-35; iii. 3-7; and throughout the pages of Joshua. Concubinage was placed under liberal appointments. When any of the chosen race had "a desire" for any "beautiful woman" taken "captive" in war, she was to be allowed a month wherein to bemoan her slaughtered parents, and then was admitted to the privileges of Hebrew prostitution, so long as might be agreeable to her captor ; and when he ceased to have "delight in her," she was to be turned out and left to her own resources (Deut. xxi. 10-14). Surely "the Lord" was with these people ! Slavery, moreover, was an institution appointed by this god (Lev. xxv. 44-46), in provident consideration of their domestic exigences. The enslaved beings, not being in allegiance to him, were of course held in no account.

An "unknown God" is not desirable (Acts xvii. 23); one who lies beyond the limits of human vision, who cannot be handled, conversed with, or brought into familiar contact ; who is invisible, intangible, unfathomable, infinite, universal. Jehovah was not such. He had, as Dr Inman enumerates, a head, nostrils and nose, eyes, ear, mouth and speech, hands, feet, bosom, back (*Ancient Faiths*, I. 259-261). He could cool himself in a garden, partake of butter, milk, and veal with one patriarch, measure strength with another in a wrestling match, and converse face to face as a confidential friend with a chosen prophet, though at one time waywardly veiling his form from him, all but the hinder parts. With his name, his local seat, his limited attributes, his partialities, and his liability to anger, hatred, jealousy, love, change of mind, and vengeance, it is for those who deny the resemblance to point out in what respect Jehovah differed from, or stood above, the surrounding idols.

The posture of the worshipers is of course an index to the character of the divinity worshiped. Was this in the case of the early leaders such as to disconnect them from the idolatrous people around them? We have first to consider Abraham, "the father of the faithful." How does he stand this test? His ancestors, as close up to himself as his father Terah, were open idolaters (Josh: xxiv. 2). Abraham turned to Jehovah, but the circumstance in no way broke off the alliance with the idolatrous stock. His own wife Sarah was of it. Then he took to Hagar and Keturah, both certainly styled concubines, but still as good as wives. Hagar was an Egyptian, and of course an idolater, and it is impossible to ascribe to Keturah a purer stock. Abraham had then to provide for his son Isaac, the special heir of the promises, in matrimony, and he did so out of the old idolatrous family in Chaldea. Isaac did the like by his elect son Jacob, who there got two wives, to whom he added two idolatrous concubines; standing to him as wives, and proving mothers of four out of the twelve tribal heads of Israel. Jacob, after over-reaching his father-in-law Laban in the matter of the division of their cattle under a suggestion obtained by him from his god, secretly withdrew with all his family and goods. Laban follows him up, and complains that his household gods had been stolen from him. Jacob does not denounce these as no gods, but offers to put to death any one of his family with whom the outraged divinities might be found (Gen. xxxi. 32). His favourite wife Rachel had them, and managed to retain them through a fraudulent expedient, worthy even of the man she owned as her husband. Jacob then progresses to the country of Jehovah. On his way angels are sent to greet the saintly traveller (Gen. xxxii. 1, 2). He afterwards encamps on the Jordan, and there the god himself comes and wrestles with him, Jacob extorting from him a blessing (Gen. xxxii. 24-30). All this while the whole household were occupied with other gods, but Jacob at length, when fairly within Jehovah's territories, thinks it time to keep to his engagement with his elected deity. He thereupon took away from them their strange gods, and "hid them" ·under a particular oak in Shechem (Gen. xxxv. 1-4). The act has as reverential an aspect as could be looked for in the disposal of the objectionable divinities. Certainly it carries with it no idea of desecration or destruction of them. The only remaining patriarch with any pretension to sanctity is Joseph, and he allied himself to the daughter of an Egyptian priest—ASNeiTH, "the *devoted* to the goddess *Neith*" (*Types of Mankind*, 114). We observe him possessed of a divining cup, and laying claim to the power of using it (Gen. xliv. 5, 15). "Pliny," as our commentators, in treating of the passage, inform us, "says that 'in this hydromantia images of the gods were called up.'" The apparition, it was alleged, was obtained by "looking into the water as into a mirror." We find him also employing Egyptian "physicians" to embalm, or make a mummy of his father (Gen. l. 2), an expedient necessary to their superstitious idea of a physical resurrection of the identical body deceased. Was he of a purer faith than they? In the end Joseph himself is mummified (Gen. l. 26). Then we have the great prophet and leader Moses. He is trained up in Egyptian lore, of course by the priesthood, the sole depositaries of the learning, and avails himself largely

of this knowledge when establishing his own ritual.
Could the teaching of the priests have been divested
of their mythological histories? He marries into an
idolatrous priestly family of another people, namely
Midian, and is seen to have made an Ethiopian or
Cushite connection (Num. xii. 1), this apparently being
a second wife.

These important followers of Jehovah were all in
intimate contact with the outside races, termed the
heathen. The Patriarchs passed their days in Canaan.
Abraham also visited Egypt. Jacob was for years in
Chaldea. Joseph's life from early youth was spent in
Egypt. Moses also was there till mid-age. If they
had a knowledge of the true God, did they attempt to
impart this to any of those around them who were
trusting in false gods? It is apparent that they made
no such effort. They lived socially with their neighbours, but sought not to lead them to Jehovah. Nor
could they consistently have done so. Jehovah had
not revealed himself to them as the God universal.
He was a god simply for themselves, the god of Abraham, Isaac, and Jacob. The other people had their
gods, and to these they left them.

Sacrifice is a gift designed to conciliate an irate or
hostile god. It is in itself a type of idolatry. "The
fear of the Lord" (Jehovah) is not "the beginning,"
but the end of "wisdom." The true God inspires confidence and love. It is only the ideal gods of human
manufacture who are exhibited to mankind as objects
of terror, who have to be approached through offerings presented to purchase their favour. The whole
Judaic system, to speak of no more modern system,
labours under this stigma, and stamps the divinity so
addressed as other than the true God. The sacrificial
exigencies render it impossible to distinguish the

worship of Jehovah from that which was offered to any neighbouring idol.

But there were peculiar forms of worship which bring the correspondence in the instance of the patriarchs closer still.

One was the phallic worship, or that of the organs of generation. The theory was that the creator combined in his own person the two sexes, and through their action brought the whole creation into being. This is the Hindu myth described by Menu (*see Beveridge's Hist. of India.*) It is the Brahma and Prakriti, united in one, of the Puranas, of whom Dr Inman gives pictorial representations (*Ancient Faiths*, II. 643-645, *plate* II. *and fig.* 44; *also Higgins' Anac.* I. 279.) The Priapus of the Etruscans was both male and female, also the Diana of Ephesus, the Urania of Persia, the Jove of Greece, and the Venus Aphrodite (*Anac.* I. 48, 70.) And the copying Hebrews had it for their representation of Jehovah.

"So God created man in his own image, in the image of God created he him; male and female created he them." That the Hebrew god had an external form is apparent, as when he feasted with Abraham, wrestled with Jacob, and showed himself to "Moses, Aaron, Nadab, Abihu, and seventy of the elders of Israel," on the holy mount (Exod. xxiv. 9, 10.) And that the image here in question was the external one is made evident by the advertence to the sexes. Had Adam and Eve been formed after the moral image of God, as commonly alleged, would they have been without even the very moderate and indispensable attribute of power to discern between good and evil? And could they have fallen under the first insignificant temptation presented to them? That the image spoken of was the external, and not an internal moral

image conferred at the creation and lost at the fall, is
made clear by the circumstance that Adam retained
this image after the fall, and procreated in it his son.
The passage I now refer to brings the whole together
in a manner that should be convincing. "This is the
book of the generations of Adam. In the day that
God created man, in the likeness of God made he him;
male and female created he them; and blessed them,
and called their name Adam, in the day when they
were created. And Adam lived an hundred and thirty
years, and begat a son in his own likeness, after his
image; and called his name Seth." (Gen. y. 1-3.)
The Phallic worship arose, as I have mentioned,
upon this idea of the generative powers of the divinity
being exercised in creation. It prevails to the present
day in India, under the symbolization of the Lingam.
In Palestine the object set up for the purpose was the
Ashērāh, mis-rendered a grove, and evidently only a solitary post or pillar. Our commentators thus describe it.

"According to the most probable derivation of the name,
the *Ashērāh* represented something that was upright, which
was fixed, or planted in the ground; hence, if it was not a
tree, it must have been some sort of upright pillar or monument" (I. 41⁵).

In treating of Exodus xxxiv. 13, they say—

"The groves. The *Ashērāh* could not have been a grove,
since it was set up 'under every green tree' (1 Ki. xiv.
23; 2 Ki. xvii. 10.) A carved image of it was set up by
Manassah (2 Ki. xxi. 7,) which was stamped to powder
by Josiah (2 Ki. xxiii. 6.)"

"And Abraham planted a grove in Beer-sheba,
and called there on the name of the Lord" (Jehovah)
(Gen. xxi. 33). The grove is אשל *eshel* a tree. The
root *ashal* signifies to be firm, strong, pressed together,
the exact meanings of *ashar*, the root of *ashērāh* the

phallic symbol. The two words are probably the
same, the "r" and the "l," moreover, in the Hebrew differing but by a stroke. Thus, אשר *ashar* and אשל *ashal.*
I have this view from a competent Hebraist. Was
the object planted by Abraham the phallic symbol?
If not, in what way could it have been associated with
his worship?

"And Jacob awaked out of his sleep, and he said,
Surely the Lord (Jehovah) is in this place; and I
knew it not. And he was afraid, and said, How dread-
ful is this place! this is none other but the house of
God, and this is the gate of heaven. And Jacob rose
up early in the morning, and took the stone that he
had put for his pillows, and set it up for a pillar, and
poured oil upon the top of it;" saying, "And this
stone, which I have set up for a pillar, shall be God's
house." (Gen. xxviii. 16-22). This was when he
was on his way to Laban, and selected the god he
was pleased to render allegiance to for value to be
received. Then, years afterwards, when he returned to
his own land with his wives and numerous progeny,
he repeated the same devotional act. "And Jacob
set up a pillar in the place where he (the god) talked
with him, even a pillar of stone: and he poured a
drink offering thereon, and he poured oil thereon"
(Gen. xxxv. 14). Was not this again the phallus? If
not, what was it?

I have said that the sacrificial offering was by way
of a gift bestowed to appease a wrathful or offended
god. The more precious the gift, the more efficaci-
ous the offering. The idea led naturally, and inevi-
tably, from the offering up of animals, to the sacrifice
of human beings, as the victims of the highest order
that could be presented. This fearful practice has
prevailed in dark days in every land, even in remote

and isolated Mexico. It was habitual in Palestine
and round about at the rites known as those of Moloch. And Jehovah legislated for it for himself.
" Notwithstanding no devoted thing, that a man shall
devote unto the Lord (Jehovah) of all that he hath,
both of man and beast, and of the field of his possession, shall be sold or redeemed ; every devoted thing
is most holy unto the Lord (Jehovah).   None devoted
which shall be devoted of men, shall be redeemed ;
but shall surely be put to death " (Lev. xxvii. 28, 29).
Accordingly, Abraham, knowing what was acceptable
to his god, prepared to offer up to him his son Isaac ;
but the god was graciously pleased in lieu to satiate
himself with the blood of a ram.   Jepthah made a rash
vow which brought in his daughter as a victim to Jehovah. David, to avert the further progress of a famine,
had seven innocent sons and grandsons of Saul "hanged
in the hill before the Lord" (Jehovah). All the enemies
of Israel were devoted to death to feed the sanguinary
propensities of Jehovah.   Thus, when there was no
question of battle strife, Joshua "hanged" the helpless
king of Ai "on a tree until eventide" (viii. 29), and
in like manner dragged from their hiding-places five
kings of the Amorites, "and slew them, and hanged
them on five trees " " until the evening " (x. 27).   And
thus the saintly Samuel, in cold blood, "hewed" the
captive "Agag in pieces before the Lord (Jehovah) in
Gilgal" (1 Sam. xv. 33).   All the first-born in Israel,
"both of man and of beast," were theoretically devoted
to propitiate Jehovah, but, happily for the human
victims, they might be redeemed by substituted
sacrifices.

How are we to distinguish the demands of Jehovah
from those of Moloch ? And are we content to have
him for our god ?

SAINTS AND SINNERS.

Nothing more clearly characterizes, and commends to our senses, the real God, than his discrimination between good and evil. His laws are so perfect, and so exquisitely adjusted, that not one of them can be violated, or disturbed, in the least degree, without entailing corresponding consequences. We may be unconscious for a time that there are such consequences, but in the end they reveal themselves. The slow, graduated, well-balanced application of measure for measure, the sum of the transgression met, as the misrule advances, with the sum of its results, masking too often, to our undiscerning minds, the progress of the retribution, till it assumes proportions that cannot be mistaken. The careless spendthrift ending in the unscrupulous bankrupt, the convivialist in the confirmed sot, the equivocator in the unblushing liar, the pilferer in the highwayman, the hasty striker in the murderer, will illustrate my meaning. And as in morals, so in the treatment of the physical frame, indiscretions, marked with consequences too trivial to arrest attention, producing by repetition on an impairing system ultimate constitutional ruin. The same rule prevails through the whole material creation. Any interference with the controlling laws is stamped with accordant results. Nor is the measure of the testimony which the true God thus gives against what is out of order, or evil, to be limited by the experiences of the present life. There is a future before us which will doubtless be still more pregnant with instruction.

Jehovah, in his dealings with his subjects, manifests the reverse of attributes such as these. He is wayward, harsh, arbitrary, undiscerning, influenced by partialities, self-seeking, and destitute of true perceptions of ends to be worked out in appointing his favours and dispensing his judgments. He is the conception of ignorant minds, setting up false standards, in days of darkness. I point to so much in the Hebrew discriminations as may serve to expose the character of their divinity.

Were it possible that such a scene as that depicted in the garden of Eden could have occurred, the true God would have caused the offence to bring with it its appropriate consequences; so much; that much with certainty and fitness of application and of measure; and no more. But Jehovah, for one act of disobedience, by persons of unformed minds, and destitute of experience, plunges a whole world, in its undeveloped bud, into measureless, and, for all but favourites, never ending ruin. I have endeavoured in my episode of "The Snake in the Grass," to make the proper estimate of this dispensation apparent.

The curse being thus liberally showered upon all, there follows a system of selection for blessing, governed by no considerations out of which we can derive any moral instruction. The apostle enters upon the discussion why, out "of the same lump," his god should have made vessels purposely "fitted to destruction," and others "prepared unto glory," and then leaves us, where he found us, without a solution (Rom. ix. 6-24). Nor is the matter explicable.

The Israelites were elected in a body as the god's chosen people. No one, I think, who studies the type, can admire the selection. Certainly their past history, as depicted by themselves, does not commend them to us as objects of regard or models to follow. Nor is the election productive of solid results. They were often liberally treated with destruction. The whole body, with two favoured exceptions, perished judicially in the wilderness, although transcendent monuments of their god's redeeming power, when brought, with so much expense of suffering to the Egyptians, out of their bondage in Egypt. More partial slaughterings, but mostly involving undiscriminated thousands, occurred from time to time in the wilderness and through the period of their history as a people in Palestine. And the end has been the rejection of the race, with the disallowance of the whole of their divinely appointed ordinances. What lesson are we to learn from such a dispensation as this? Is the god, so electing, and so breaking through the election, one to whom we should like to commit ourselves?

Then there were the specially accepted ones, and those specially visited for transgressions.

Enoch, though a lost sinner, was so very perfect, that he was translated to heaven without even tasting of death. It would have been instructive to have had put before us the considerations by which he chose his path in those early times. We only know that he "walked with God," which possibly means no more than that he was true to Jehovah.

The human race being tainted with sin from the act of their first progenitors, and abandoned to themselves without redeeming grace or inspired revelation, could scarcely have progressed in any other course than that course of sin marked out for them. The wrath of the god at length boiled over, and he resolved to destroy them all, repenting that he had ever made them. But one single man stood out as righteous in his sight. This was Noah, of whose merits all we know is that he too "walked with God." The inspired historian fails of material when he has to describe what constitutes a holy walk. It is not pretended that his family, consisting of seven persons, were on a like footing of holiness with himself, but the discriminative god let them into the ark of salvation, apparently to keep up the stock, as in the selected brute creation couples. The patriarch is no sooner safe on dry land than he intoxicates himself, exposes his person in an unseemly manner, and because then inspected by a son, curses for the indiscretion one of that son's sons, and his future descendants. What lesson are we to draw from this divine selection?

A fresh election was made in Abraham. This was purely arbitrary, there being no pretence that a "walking with God" led thereto. On the contrary, Abraham must previously have walked with the paternal idols; nor can we see that he passed into a purer element of worship. We find him involved in the rites of Moloch and the phallic worship. He is ready twice to sacrifice the virtue of his wife for his personal safety. Not above the manners of the day, he accepts a harlot of his wife's appointment, and at his wife's bidding, and the instigation of his god, he turns her and her son out to perish in the desert. His lawful son he is prepared to sacrifice at the shrine of his divinity. He is presented to us as the father of the faithful. Would we like to tread in any one of his footsteps?

Here we have the episode of Lot, in whom, as in

Noah, centred another important and typical salvation. He was the one righteous man whom the god could lay his hand upon in Sodom. But when we wish to know how he manifested his righteousness in that corrupt city, we are left as uninstructed as in the parallel case of the accepted Noah. And for the sake of his righteousness, as in the instance of the earlier patriarch, his family, sinners as they were, were saved with him. One, however, speedily proved to be a wrong selection. The wife ventured to look back upon her burning home. Perhaps, in her secret soul, she regretted, or even condemned, the manifestation, in this shape, of the wrath of Jehovah. She, consequently, was left on the spot, turned into a pillar of salt. Let us occupy ourselves with the saved ones. At the outset, Lot was desirous of thrusting out for misuse by a lascivious crowd his virgin daughters. It is needless to speak of the justifying cause, as for such an act there could be no justification. Then they are saved, the father and the two daughters. What they did together I must leave it to the Bible to describe.

We get to Isaac. All we know of him is, that he walked in the paternal footsteps in his readiness to prostitute his wife for his own preservation, and in seeking a yoke fellow for his son from the circle of his idolatrous ancestry. Of Jacob more is told, but there is nothing that we can see to his advantage. Promiscuous idolatry prevailed in his household till he felt it safe to ally himself singly to Jehovah. This worship he could celebrate with phallic symbols. His personal character is simply odious, marked with fraud of his father, fraud of his brother Esau, fraud of his uncle Laban, and cowardice throughout.

Of Joseph we know little. He had the merit of

chastity, but in his posture stands out merely as an Egyptian. He marries the daughter of a priest of that people, and could scarcely but have conformed himself to their ways. He uses the magic art of divination and trusts in mummifying.

The merit of Moses is his devotion to Jehovah, and his national sentiment. His legislative enactments and ordinances were largely derived from Pagan sources, and then palmed off as original revelations from his god. His coarse and brutal legislation bespeaks a corresponding mind.

Samuel is our next saintly character. He was zealous for Jehovah, as he proved upon the person of the unhappy Agag. In himself, in all that is given us to judge by, he is manifested as an ambitious priest, loth to part with the rule exercised by him, and when superseded by an elected king, domineering over his sovereign. That he did so in the name of Jehovah is unfortunately no evidence of the purity of his motives.

Elijah is a figure so prominent for holiness as to have been translated to the celestial regions, as was Enoch, without undergoing death. How these could have shaken themselves free of the results of the primeval curse is of course a great question, but it remains unanswered. We can only perceive in him an earnest follower of Jehovah, as he proved himself upon the four hundred and fifty priests of the rival Baal, whom he treated, not with argument, but the sword. Do we learn any wholesome lesson here?

Of the saintly David, the man after the god's own heart, it is difficult to speak except in terms of abhorrence. We find him, after being a favourite at court, standing in rebellion against his king, surrounded by a band of needy and discontented adventurers. The king may have been most in the wrong in the quarrel, but the character of David's associates stamps with degradation his own position. What that position was becomes the more apparent when he comes into action. When Nabal declined to respond to his levies, this righteous man meditated putting him and all his to the sword. He was turned from his purpose by Nabal's wife, persuasive in the goodness of her looks and the cleverness of her speech. The saint was very susceptible to attractions of this kind. Nabal departs this life mysteriously a few days after this occurrence, and Abigail passes over to the saint's seraglio. Then he accepts the hospitality of the king of Gath, and professing to go out on forages against the king's enemies, falls upon and exterminates his allies. The saint is careful not to let one soul escape to report his treachery. He had managed, so well did he act his part, to exhibit himself to his confiding and deluded entertainer "as an angel of God," (1 Sam. xxix. 9). He had previously passed himself off to him as a drivelling idiot. That he could do so much damage, and not even fall under suspicion, certainly does not support the veracity of the history. After years of contest with the rightful heir, through warfare and intrigue, David gains his throne. He fills his seraglio with women, wives and concubines, and both in abundance, and yet covets the wife of his faithful Uriah, whom he circumvents by sending him to his grave. Then he appropriates his prize, having already held adulterous intercourse with her. When he overcomes his enemies, he slaughters them, according to the custom of the chosen people, in cold blood. The Moabites are thrown to the ground and measured with a line, and "with two lines measured he to put to

death, and with one full line to keep alive" (2 Sam.
viii. 2). When he took Rabbah, "He brought forth
the people that were therein, and put them under saws,
and under harrows of iron, and under axes of iron, and
made them pass through the brick-kiln. And thus
did he unto all the cities of the children of Ammon"
(2 Sam. xii. 31). And when he subdued Edom, he
left his general, Joab, to execute his will, and "for six
months did Joab remain there with all Israel until he
had cut off every male in Edom" (1 Ki. xi. 16). The
sacrifice of Saul's sons and grandsons, I have already
adverted to. It was perpetrated in violation of his
oath to Saul that he would not "cut off his seed after
him" (1 Sam. xxiv. 21, 22). Jehovah became
appeased, consenting "after that" to be "intreated
for the land" (2 Sam. xxi. 14). At length the saintly
king approached his last moments. He had become
"old and stricken in years." His servants were
unable to restore heat to his body by covering.
Then, knowing his propensities, they sought out for
him the fairest damsel they could meet with in all
Israel, and laid her by his side. But it was too late.
The old monarch's powers had sunk too far to be
even thus revivified. What a picture of a dying
saint Bible-drawn! His latest breath was used in
displacing his lawful heir, to exalt to the throne the
son of the adulterous wife he had wrenched from
Uriah. And to him he committed his last wishes,
which were, that he should murder his two personal
enemies, Shimei, whose life he had sworn to spare
(2 Sam. xix. 23), and Joab his general, who had
served him so well, but of whom he stood in awe;
a testament which his divinely endowed heir faithfully executed. Then we have the inspired estimate

of this model king. Jehovah had looked into his "heart," and found him perfect in all his ways, "save only" in that little "matter of Uriah the Hittite," (1 Ki. xv. 3-5).

Transgressions against morals are, we see, lightly esteemed, but to violate the majesty of Jehovah touched him personally, and was a deadly offence. So it proved in the case of Lot and his party. The drunkenness and incest of the saved persons were passed over, but the silent remonstrance against the judgment of Jehovah, expressed by the wife by a mere attitude, converted her into an awful monument of destruction. This test of a false god runs through the visitations of Jehovah.

Cain, the murderer, escapes judgment. David and Solomon, equally guilty, are honoured. But to worship Jehovah with strange fire entailed a visitation by celestial fire (Lev. x. 1, 2); one who ventured, against his ceremonial ordinance, to pick up sticks on the sabbath day, is stoned to death (Num. xv. 32-36); the earth opens upon Korah, Dathan, Abiram, and fire from heaven consumes their following of 250 princes, for invading the priestly office of Aaron (Num. xvi. 1-35); 14,700 men of the congregation of Israel are smitten to death for daring even to murmur against Moses and Aaron (Num. xvi. 41-49); Achan and all his family are judicially executed for his individual act in appropriating booty against the divine command (Josh. vii. 24, 25); 50,070 men of Beth-shemesh are struck dead for daring to look into the sacred ark (1 Sam. vi. 19), "Who," it is then exclaimed, "is able to stand before this holy god Jehovah!" Who indeed! On Uzzah putting his hand out to steady the sacred receptacle, when shaken upon a cart, the offended god smites him to death (2 Sam. vi. 6, 7). And for David's incomprehensible transgression in numbering Israel, 70,000 men, guiltless of the offence, perish (2 Sam. xxiv. 10-17).

Is not the character of this Jehovah, as a humanly devised imitation god, proclaimed in these his estimates of saints and sinners?

IN the authorised version of the Bible, the precise year in which the globe we inhabit was formed is laid down as being B.C. 4004. This gives the earth an age at the present time of 5875 years. The race of man, begun in Adam, is said to have been cut off at the flood, the date stated for which is B.C. 2349. The age of man upon the earth, therefore, as renewed in Noah, is now 4220 years. Such is the Bible account.

Facts, however, elicited by modern research, quarrelled violently with assertions such as these, and the supporters of the Bible have been driven to unworthy devices to maintain the integrity of the record. In the earlier days, when the knowledge they had to meet was more immature than it is at this day, they were proportionately bolder in their allegations offered on the defence. Leaders are expected to be courageous, and one accordingly stepped forward to meet the difficulty. "This," said Dr Chalmers, "is a false alarm. The writings of Moses do not fix the antiquity of the globe." Had his object been the pursuit of truth in the abstract, and not merely of Bible truth, he could have made no such unfounded assertion. But having thrown aside the scruples which should have governed him, his next step was to make use of imagination for fact. He was constrained to acknowledge, in recognition of the revelations of the geologists, a long era of creation not revealed by Moses. But this he said had closed with a streak of death passing over it, obliterating all that had gone before, on the top of which was produced the creation of Moses. Should such a solution have been satisfactory to any pure and discerning mind? Moses undertook to describe, not the creation of the superficies of the earth, nor the creation of the earth, in any sense, alone, but the creation of "the heaven and the earth," and "*all* that in them is." Could he properly have omitted to mention the existence of the earth and sun, to say no more, in long prior ages, together with what had been then produced in the earth? During these ages terrestrial operations were carried on in the deposition of stratified rocks, and in depressions and upheavals of land and water, the lands being turned into beds of oceans, and beds of oceans into dry land ; and the whole was stocked with vegetation and animal life, in every aspect, marine and terrestrial, as we now have it—from seaweed to the highest forms of forest growth; from mollusks to fishes, reptiles, birds, and mammals. To discover the traces of these operations and products unmentioned by Moses, and to see him coming forward with a new and recent beginning for all these things as being the first opening of their existence, is to expose Moses as an unreliable narrator. But the Bibliolater will not be silenced. He will have his record whether he is to stand upon his heels or his head to peruse it. And so Dr Chalmers strove to shelter Moses with the prior obliteration or streak of death. Here also he thought he had the much needed chaos. Other leading minds gladly accepted his solution. They fancied it assured to them foundations still to stand upon. Among these were Dr Buckland and Hugh Miller. But the geologists went on with their investigations. They ascertained that there had been no such streak of death, and no such chaos. The crust of the earth, to the depth of about fourteen miles, has been seen to be laid out in a well ordered series of deposits, and to have been stocked throughout with products vegetable and animal. The earth was not therefore left, when taken up by Moses, "without form and void" as represented by him. It exhibits no chaos prior to his creation. Nor did a streak of death occur as alleged by Dr Chalmers on the basis of his imagination. All that has passed has been interlaced with all that exists. The earliest forms are repeated in the present ones in a never ending upward development, without break or interruption. Hugh Miller, in prosecution of his researches as a geologist, came, among others, to discover that it was so, and then, to save the Bible from sinking into the mire yielding under his feet, he had to shift his ground, and to seek some other basis on which to maintain a footing. Again the imagination was resorted to as the instrument for the presentation of fact. The days of the creation of Moses were no more, as hitherto, natural days, but were converted, to meet the exigency, into ages. The word in fact was altered. A Bibliolater shows us, at every turn, that he will hesitate at nothing to support his creed (*Testimony of the Rocks, preface, and pp.* 113-123).

Our commentators appear to accept the words of Moses in their natural signification. The days of creation are with them ordinary days. The geologists, for the present, they leave to themselves. They do not attract attention to their revelations. The science is in its infancy, and they hope in the future for some deliverance from the present difficulties. What they are concerned about is the short era given by Moses.

for the age of man, as against the perception dawning
upon them that he has had a much longer era.   For
this they felt themselves bound to suggest some
remedy, and the best that has occurred to them is a
possible, and an indefinite, stretching of the genealogies.   Let us see to what limits this process will
have to be carried.

The earliest personage of whom we have knowledge
from secular sources is Menes, the first king of Manetho's first dynasty.   According to the figures of
Manetho, as read off by Mariette Bey, he reigned
B.C. 5004 (*Aperçu de L'Histoire Ancienne D'Egypte*, 65).
The estimate of Lepsius is that the time was B.C.
3893 (*Nott and Gliddon's Types of Mankind*, 236).
Both eras long precede the deluge.   Wilkinson, "for
fear of interfering with the deluge," placed this reign
at B.C. 2201, removed from the alleged event but by
148 years.   Afterwards he was led to date it at B.C.
2700, or 351 years before that event (*Types of Mankind*, 683).   This last was a great stretch of liberality
on the part of a thoroughly orthodox man.

Mariette Bey allows that nothing like certainty of
date can be obtained from Manetho's tables till we
arrive at the 26th dynasty in B.C. 665, owing to altera-
tions and negligence by the christian hands through
whom the record has been transmitted to us (*Aperçu*,
68-70).   The method of those to whom it would be
convenient to discredit Manetho altogether, is to suggest that he has described contemporaneous families
of kings, ruling in various divisions of the Egyptian
territories, as successional dynasties; but from this
charge Mariette Bey successfully defends him.   He
finds evidences, in the monumental remains, of families
of rulers, to whom Manetho gives no place, which, had

he been guilty of multiplying dynasties as successional, would not have been overlooked by him. He might, it appears, have in this way presented us with sixty dynasties, instead of confining himself to thirty-one. And the monumental evidences further show particular families to have been successional, which the objectors have sought to double up as collateral (*Aperçu*, 66-68).

At some remote age, then, and probably·centuries before the era of the alleged deluge, reigned Menes. In what condition stood Egypt, at that time, as respects those arts which are the stamp of a people advanced in knowledge or the reverse?

Mariette Bey, as do all Egyptologists, places the monumental remains in distinct groups. He puts together those of the dynasties one to three; then those of the fourth and fifth dynasties; then those of the sixth dynasty; and then those of the eleventh and onwards. The era of the dynasties from seven to ten was one of internal strife and trouble, and produced no such remains. The works traceable to the earliest division are but few, consisting of one of the pyramids of·Saccara, the tomb of Tot-hotep, and three statues·connected with Sepa. A table of kings found at Saccara amply supports Manetho in the names laid down by him in these early dynasties. Where Manetho thus most required support, he has it (*Aperçu*, 75, 76). But it is in the works ascribed to the next dynasties, namely the fourth and fifth, said to have ruled from B.C. 4235 to 3951, that Egyptian art most excelled. These are, (1) the great pyramids of Gizeh, which are of the 4th dynasty; (2) magnificent tombs here and at Saccara; (3) a temple in alabaster and granite found near the great Sphinx at Gizeh; (4) a statue of Chephren, the founder of the second·pyramid,

described as majestic and highly finished in its details;
(5) an inscription showing that Khoufou, the founder
of the first pyramid, had presented temple offerings of
images of stone, gold, bronze, ivory, and wood ; (6)
a grand monumental column found at the pyramids of
Gizeh, in which the names of Snéfrou II., Khoufou,
and Chephren are recorded ; (7) a wooden statue, the
features of which are said to be admirably represented;
(8) beautifully executed sarcophaguses in red and
dark granites ; (9) and a large collection of monumental tablets and statues, which have been deposited
in the museum of Boulac. Manetho's account of these
dynasties again receives support from the Table of
Saccara (*Aperçu*, 76-78).   The renewal of art from the
11th dynasty onwards was of a decidedly inferior
order to what belongs to the prior dynasties.

It is thus apparent that at the remote age when
we hear of these early rulers in Egypt, the arts
and sciences had advanced to a degree so high as to
bear comparison with the efforts of the present day.
In some respects they remain unapproached, as in the
construction of the pyramids, which are monuments of
perfection in scientific construction and application of
mechanical power.   Although the records may be
wanting, there undoubtedly existed a long era of civi-
lisation, either in Egypt, or in some parent region whence
the occupants of Egypt emigrated, anterior to Menes.

Among the remains of the twelfth dynasty, said to
have been of B.C. 3064, we have pictures distinguishing
the features of races foreign to the Egyptians, namely
other Asiatics, and the African negroes (*Types of Mankind*, 171-180); and there is a tablet of the time of
Sesourtesen III. of this dynasty, discovered in Nubia
by Viscount de Rougé, showing that this king had ex-

tended his bounds to the third cataract, and took steps to repress the advances of his enemies beyond that point. The inscription is this: "Frontier of the south. Done in the year VIII., under Sesourtesen (III.), ever-living; in order that it may not be permitted to any *negro* to pass by it navigating" (down the river.) (*Types of Mankind*, 268, 269). If mankind sprang, as the Bible states, from a common stock, a period which may not be estimated, but one evidently of enormous magnitude, must have elapsed, to have produced the marked characteristics of the negro; but here we have the type already existing at a date, taking the chronologies to be approachably true, more than 700 years before the renewed parentage in Noah.

The Pagan mythologies on all sides were associated with the powers of nature, and especially with the heavenly orbs. Astronomy was a science intimately cultivated at a very early period. I give a few prominent dates of early labours in this field, derived from Chambers' Descriptive Astronomy.

About B.C. 125 Hipparchus discovered that movement termed the precession of the equinoxes. He did so on comparisons of observations made by Timocharis and Aristyllus about 178 years previously.

B.C. 323-283. This is the age of Euclid, the author of the Elements of Geometry, still our school-book.

B.C. 450. Diogenes referred the change of the seasons to the inclination of the axis of the earth.

B.C. 584. Thales predicted a solar eclipse of that year.

B.C. 719, 720. Three lunar eclipses observed in Babylon, as mentioned by Ptolemy.

B.C. 1100. The obliquity of the ecliptic observed by Tcheou-king in China, as mentioned by Laplace.

B.C. 2127. A solar eclipse described in the Chinese history called Chou-king, which is supposed to be the eclipse of the 13th October of that year.

Mr S. A. Mackey (*Mythological Astronomy*, 68), says that Calisthenes, when in Babylon with Alexander the Great (B.C. 331), was furnished by Berossus, the historian of the Babylonians, with astronomical calculations that had been made during a past series of 1903 years, which brings us to the epoch of B.C. 2234, or within 115 years of the Noachic deluge.

The precession of the equinoxes is a movement caused by the attraction of the sun and the moon at the equator. The earth's diameter is there widest by nearly twenty-six and a half miles, and the sun and the moon acting in greater force upon this protuberant mass, draw the poles out of position and cause them to perform a very slow circular movement, independent of the diurnal rotation of the earth upon its axis. The shifting of the stars from their recorded places, as observed from time to time, led to the discovery of the fact of such a movement. My diagram No. 1 is to illustrate this action. The line of the ecliptic represents the course held by the earth in its orbit round the sun. It is along that line that the earth faces the sun as it traverses its path. The equator lies at an angle therewith, and where the two meet, on either side of the sphere of the earth, the equinoxes occur. That is, when the earth in its course faces the sun at these points, the sunlight is spread over half the earth, producing in all parts of it equal days and nights. This occurs twice in the year, at spring and autumn, giving us a vernal and an autumnal equinox. The circle of the ecliptic is divided into twelve portions, which constitutes the

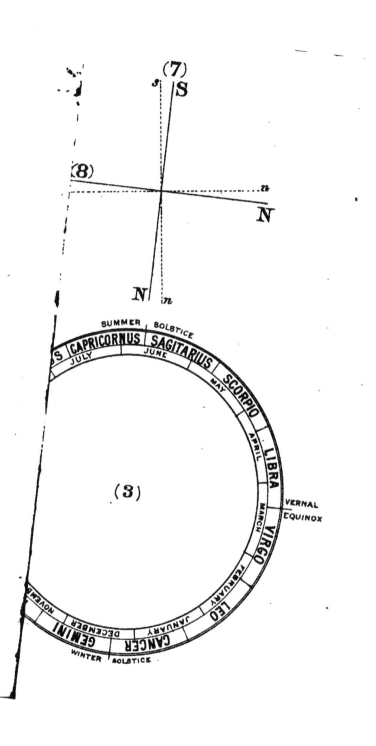

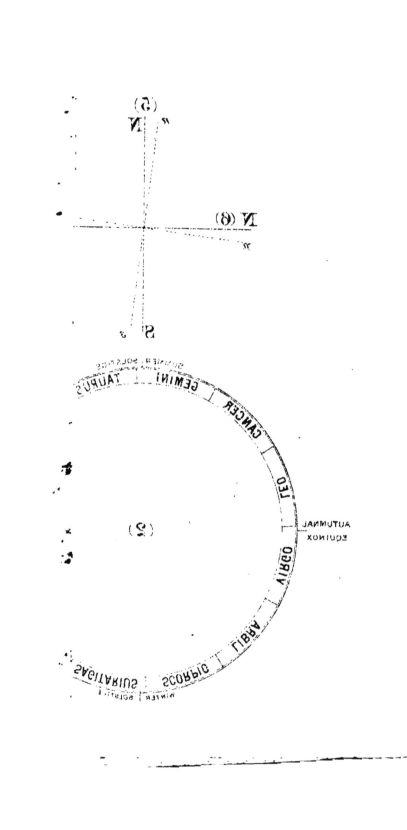

INDIAN ZODIAC.

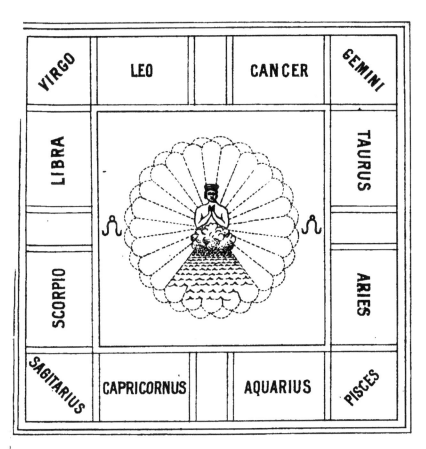

VIRGO LEO CANCER GEMINI

LIBRA TAURUS

SCORPIO ARIES

SAGITARIUS CAPRICORNUS AQUARIUS PISCES

AS EXHIBITED IN THE

PHILOSOPHICAL TRANSACTIONS

FOR 1772.

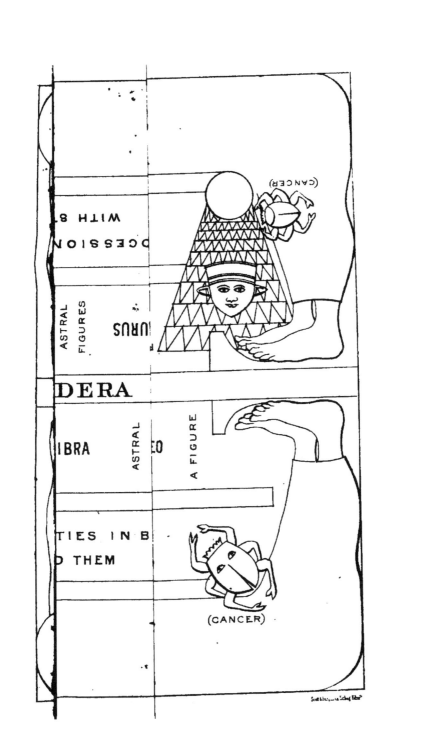

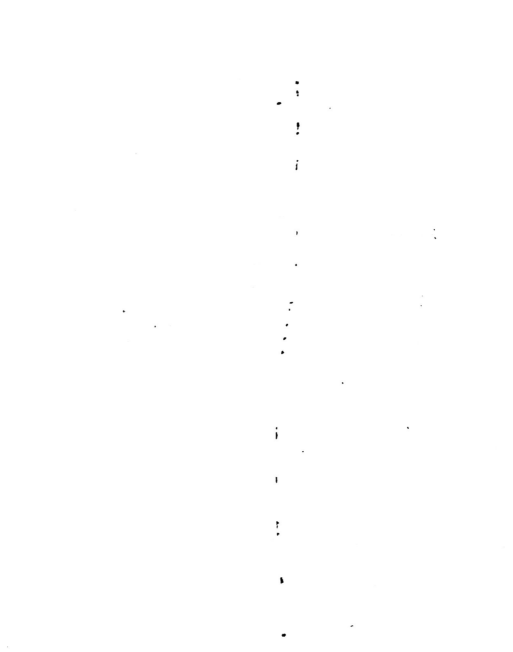

zodiac, each portion being distinguished by an appointed sign. The circular movement of the poles,
before mentioned, causes a perpetual shifting of the
equinoctial points, whereby we get the term by which
the operation is known of the precession of the equinoxes. Now it is evident that a zodiac drawn at one
time will not be true at another distant time. Zodiacs, as thus compared, become therefore registers of
the passage of time.

The period occupied in the complete revolution
of the signs of the zodiac is commonly given as
25,868 years. A precise calculation has been communicated to me showing it to be 25,810.6 years,
by which I think it safe to go. Denison (*Astronomy
without Mathematics*, 31) reduces the period to
20,984 years by combining therewith a movement
arising from the eliticity of the earth's axis, termed
the revolution of the apsides, but I do not find this
practically followed by others. Taking then 25,810
years to be the time, 2,150 years may be said to be
occupied by each sign.

The sun's place at the vernal equinox this year, I
am informed, was at 1° 19′ 48″·8 in Pisces, showing
that when he has made a further passage of about a
a degree and twenty seconds, involving a lapse of
about ninety-five years, Aquarius will be brought to
the equinox. My diagram 2 represents the zodiac in
this its present position.

There are two zodiacs at Dendera, a circular and
an oblong one, given in plates XLVIII. and XLIX.
attached to Denon's Voyages dans l'Egypte. Denon,
it may be noticed, was a savant attached to the
expedition of the first Napoleon. In these, Cancer is
supposed to be in the zenith or summer solstice, and

the passage of time they indicate is therefore insufficient to require notice.

The zodiac of Esne is of greater antiquity.   It is
described in the Penny Cyclopædia, and by Sir Wm.
Drummond (*Œdipus Judaicus*, lii.), who gives a
drawing from it.   The signs are placed in two lines, at
the head of one of which is Leo, supposed to be in
the ascendant, and at the head of the other is Virgo
as descending.   The zenith would lie between them,
and the vernal equinox would stand at the line between Gemini and Taurus.   This implies a retrogression of three signs, less 1° 20′, from the places the
signs now occupy, which gives a past period of 6,355
years.   Sir Wm. Drummond (lxvi.) goes rather beyond this, estimating the age of this zodiac as being
about 6,450 years when he wrote, which was in 1811.

Dupuis (*Origine de tous les Cultes*, III. 352) mentions
a still older zodiac, of India, as described in the
"Transactions Philosophiques."   Drummond has a
drawing thereof, from which I have made the accom-
panying design.   This is quadrilateral in form, and
in it Virgo, besides having her position among the
signs, is repeated and placed in the centre surrounded
by rays, whence it is inferred that this sign stands in
the zenith. .   Assuming the place of the zenith to be
the middle of the sign, the vernal equinox would
occur in the middle of Gemini, making this zodiac
older by the period of half a sign than that of Esne,
which gives it the age of 7,430 years.

The signs are of the same number, and substantially of the same forms, in the zodiacs of Egypt,
India, Persia, Phœnicia, Greece, and Italy (*Dupuis*,
III. 361).   The palm of antiquity necessarily lies between Egypt and India.   These countries approach

each other in various points connected with their legends and mythologies, but here, whichever of the two is the older nation, in the matter of the zodiac Egypt appears to have given the lead. Had the zodiac originated in India, their most important animal, the elephant, which appears in their independent lunar zodiac, would scarcely have failed to secure a place (*Higgins' Anacalypsis*, I. 3, 308). Dupuis (III. 328-339) has an argument throwing great light on this subject. The signs, he observes, have been chosen with a significancy, and certain of them evidently denote seasons of the year. Thus Taurus, it has been held, represents the time of ploughing, and Virgo, with sheaves of corn in her hands, obviously refers to the harvest. In Egypt, and in the East generally, these operations occur in November and March. Placing the signs in question in correspondence with these months, as in my diagram 3, Capricorn, Aquarius, and Pisces, appear at the months of July, August, and September. Capricorn is always associated with a fish, his form generally ending in a fish's tail. These three signs, consequently, indicate some operation connected with water, and at the months in question occur the inundations of the Nile. Dupuis naturally assumes that these correspondences make it evident that the signs originated in Egypt, and at the same time demonstrate that the zodiac, so provided, must have been invented when these signs stood at the months proper to them.

My diagram 3 gives the zodiac in this position, the particular points of the signs being so placed as to represent the solstices and equinoxes as occurring on the 21st or 23d of the months respective to them. The vernal equinox stands there on the line between

Libra and Virgo, which involves a difference of nearly
seven signs from its present place. The lapse of
time is 14,955 years.

That such was the position of the zodiac at the
time of the first adoption of the signs, is supported
by the oblong zodiac of Dendera to which I have
before referred. I give a sketch of this zodiac
made from Denon's design. The signs here occur
in two lines, over each of which is spread the figure
of the goddess Neith. When thus represented she
symbolises the vault of heaven (*Sharpe's Egyp. Myth.*
54). Here therefore we have the two hemispheres,
each containing its zodiacal signs. At the head of
Neith are discs, one at each hemisphere, being apparently the solar orb, but here denuded of rays. At
the head of one column, near the head of the goddess,
and in a line also with one of the discs in question, is
Capricorn, followed by Sagitarius, Scorpio, Libra,
Virgo, and Leo. On the opposite column, but somewhat removed from the head of Neith, is Aquarius,
followed by Pisces, Aries, Taurus, and Gemini.
Cancer appears on both lines on or close to the legs of
Neith, near her feet. The zodiac so drawn manifestly
designates Capricorn at the zenith and Cancer at the
Nadir. It is so read by Mackay (*Myth. Astr.* 30), and
seemingly so by Dupuis (*Or. de tous les Cultes* III, 345),
following Kirker's Œdip. But the disc of the sun
is again placed at one of the figures of Cancer, and
here it is shedding forth rays of light, and is associated
with a human countenance, probably that of the sun-
god Osiris. It may be judged therefore that when
this zodiac was framed, Cancer was in the zenith, while
when the signs were originally arranged, that place was
held by Capricorn. We get thus a remarkable confir-

mation of Dupuis' interesting argument, and in this manner obtain evidence of the existence of mankind on earth, keeping to our figures, 10,735 years before the alleged deluge, and in a position of advanced knowledge sufficient for him to have composed and used a zodiac.

In the above calculation it is assumed that the zodiac was invented on the first occasion when Capricorn stood at the zenith. But possibly that was not the case, and the invention may have occurred at some previous revolution of the signs. The quadrilateral Indian zodiac given by Drummond makes it appear that such in truth was the fact. This zodiac corresponds in character with the oblong zodiac of Dendera in having its signs so arranged as to represent the zenith at one point and the sun's actual place at another. It is just as if now a zodiac were drawn combining the astronomical with the true ordering of the signs. The astronomical zodiac, framed probably about the time of Hipparchus, the discoverer of the precession of the equinoxes, would have the vernal equinox at the first degree of Aries, while the actual position would have to be shown as in the second degree of Pisces. In the Indian zodiac now in question, the signs, it will be observed, are marshalled so as to place the zenith on the line between Cancer and Leo, while Virgo, where the sun is indicated to be, appears in a corner as the second of the descending signs. It may then fairly be supposed that the zenith, as drawn, marks the order of the signs as they were at the introduction of the zodiac into India, while the place of the sun is where he stood when this particular zodiac was framed. In fact, no other explanation of the arrangements of this zodiac presents itself. Now to take Virgo, in the middle of the sign, to the place of the zenith, as here represented, would require a passage of ten and a half signs, involving the lapse of 22,575 years; and then to adjust the signs to the primitive Egyptian zodiac, would require a further retrogression of three and a half signs, occupying 7,525 years, and carrying the invention of the zodiac back to a period of over 30,000 years.

I now turn to other sources of information.

Dr Bennet Dowler, in cuttings made in the delta of the Mississippi at New Orleans, found cypress forests, of successive growths, overlying each other. Under the second forest were remains of pottery, estimated to indicate a past period of 28,000 years, as necessary to allow of the growth and decay of these forests, and under the fourth forest were human bones, in the same way computed to be of the age of 57,600 years (*Types of Mankind*, 272, 337, 338).

Of recent years the discovery of celts, or heads of weapons made of chipped flints, has opened out evidence of a far greater antiquity for man. These, with other relics of man, have been found in caves and fluvial drift deposits, in contact with the bones of extinct mammalia, such as the cave hyena, the primeval elephant, a certain species of rhinoceros, and the cave bear, carrying us back to a period too remote to be estimated.

The first known discovery of this kind was made by Mr Conyers, near Gray's Inn Lane, in 1715. It was of a large flint spear head, with which was an elephant's tooth. The next was by Mr Frere who found celts in a gravel pit at Horne in Suffolk in 1800, with bones of extinct animals (*Lubbock's Pre-historic Times*, 271). After this followed similar discoveries by MM. Toornal and Christol in the south of France in 1828, by Dr

Schmerling near Liege in Belgium in 1833 and 1834, by Mr Godwin Austen in Kent's Hole, near Torquay, in 1840, and by M. Boucher de Perthes in sand near Abbeville in 1841 (*Pre-hist. Times*, 257, 258, 268). Subsequently a host of explorers operated, among whom appear the names of Falconer, Pengelly, Prestwich, Busk, Dawkins, Fuhlrott, Rigollot, Evans, and others, through whom this branch of evidence has become copious and convincing. I will notice some of the most prominent of these discoveries.

Fragmentary human bones have been frequently found in position with the remains of the extinct mammalia, but only two skulls have been obtained capable of restoration, one discovered by Dr Schmerling in the cave of Engis, near Liege, and the other by Dr Fuhlrott in the Neanderthal, near Dusseldorf. The evidence that the latter skull belonged to the period of these mammals is, according to Sir John Lubbock, not satisfactory.

" In the Engis cave, eight miles S.W. of Liege, fragments of three human bodies (chiefly skulls) were found. The now celebrated Engis skull lay buried five feet deep in the mud beneath the alabaster covering, along with a rhinoceros tooth and reindeer bones" (*Lesley's Man's Origin and Destiny*, 54).

" As regards the Engis skull, there seems no reason to doubt that it really belonged to a man who was contemporaneous with the mammoth, the cave-bear, and other extinct mammalia." Professor Huxley, it is noticed, has well observed that these remains belong to " an epoch more distant from the age of the *Elephas primigenius*, than that is from us" (*Pre-historic Times*, 332).

In 1858 Mr Prestwich and Dr Falconer explored a cave at Brixham, three or four miles west of Torquay.

"No human bones were found, but many flint knives,
chiefly in the lowest part of the red loam, one of the most
perfect having 13 feet of bone-dirt over it, and some of them
found directly underneath the extinct forms embedded in the
stalagmite covering, and therefore necessarily of an older
age. To add certainty to the date, a perfect knife was found
close to and on a level with the hind leg of a cave-bear,
which had all its parts arranged in such complete order, that
they must have been held together by the tissues, when they
were floated into their resting-place beside the knife" (*Man's
Origin and Destiny*, 59). "As then," observes Sir J. Lubbock, speaking of these bones, "they must have been deposited soon after the death of the animal, it follows that, if
man and the cave-bear were not contemporaneous, the cave-
bear was the more recent of the two" (*Pre-historic Times*,
260).

The cave-bear is found to be the most ancient of
these extinct animals.

In 1864 Dr Falconer, in company with MM. Lartet
and de Verneuil, discovered in the valley of Vezère
pieces of ivory, on which was engraved the head seemingly of a mammoth. From the same valley M. de Vibraye brought to light the engraving on a fragment of
reindeer bone of the head of the true elephant, differing
materially from the African and Asiatic types, and in
other diggings at Dordogne and Charente he discovered, depicted on various substances, representations
of a combat of reindeer, of a stag and doe, a horse,
ox, otter, and beaver, all designed with artistic skill,
and indicating a knowledge of these animals in life.
The fossil bones of these animals were in the same
localities (*Man's Or. and Dest.*, 258-261).

Thus, in those incalculably remote ages, we see
traces, not merely of man's existence, but that he

commanded instruments and skill to execute works of art, the faithfulness of which can be appreciated at the present day. <u>The remarkable features of the cave of Aurignac, in the south of France, introduce us apparently to the type of his religion.</u>

One of the earliest forms of worship met with is the reverence paid to ancestors. This must be taken as a demonstration of hope in a future state, where the worshipers believe they are to join the objects venerated. Such expectation appears expressed in the very interesting remains at Aurignac.

A peasant, named Bonnemaison, who in 1852 was occupied in making a terrace for a vineyard, " seeing a rabbit run into a hole on a steep slope, put his hand in, and, to his surprise, pulled out a human bone." He then came upon a large stone slab, set upright against a small arched opening, on removing which seventeen human skeletons were discovered together with mammalian teeth and eighteen little discs of sea-shell pierced as for ornamental use. In 1860 M. Lartet visited the spot. The human remains had been removed and buried, and he failed to succeed in tracing them out. Over the floor of the grotto, and on a terrace level with it in front, was a continuous deposit containing " hearthstones, charred wood, and beds of cinders, pottery, flint tools, arrow-heads, and burned and fractured bones of animals," namely, of " the great cave-bear, the mammoth, the rhinoceros, the great horned Irish elk, and the cave-lion, attesting the immense antiquity of the event ;" and these had been " split lengthwise" for the marrow, and " gnawed by hyenas," demonstrating that when so deposited they were fresh and capable of use as food. There were no such gnawed remains within the grotto, the

slab that protected its entrance having kept out the
depredators. Here, within the grotto, was the whole
limb of a cave-bear, on which the flesh must have
existed when deposited. There were also within the
grotto human bones, flint flakes, a kind of hammer,
bones and horns of reindeer shaped as awls, bodkins,
arrow-heads, and whetstones, and also a bird's head
formed out of the eye-tooth of a bear. In the earth
thrown out when the human skeletons were removed
were discovered " a beautiful specimen of worked reindeer horn," a hundred flints many so small as to represent merely "miniature weapons," also human bones,
bones of animals not broken or gnawed, and several
fragments of pottery. The conclusion formed has
been that this was a funerary grotto, food and models
of their weapons being supplied to the dead, according to known usage in later times, and funeral feasts
held in their honour outside the place of sepulture
(*Man's Orig. and Dest.,* 261-264 ; *Pre-hist. Times,* 262-
265 ; *Lyell's Antiquity of Man,* 181-193).

The most important results yet obtained in proof of
the great antiquity of the human race come from
Kent's Cavern, where explorations for the last seven
years have been systematically conducted by a Committee of the British Association under the personal
supervision of two of the members, Messrs Vivian
and Pengelly. The latter has been good enough to
supply me with the Annual Reports of the Committee,
and has brought to my notice a treatise on this subject
published in Chambers's Miscellany, from which sources
I now draw.

The cavern has six distinct deposits, which are—
(1) black mould; (2) a floor of stalagmite; (3) a
black band ; (4) cave earth ; (5) an older floor of

stalagmite; (6) breccia. In the black mould are mediæval, Romano-British, and pre-Roman remains, consisting of pottery, bronze articles, bone and flint tools, and human bones and bones of animals, not, however, embracing any of the extinct tribes. This is the existing floor of the cavern, and of a comparatively modern era. The deposits, 2, 3, and 4, contain flint tools and bones of extinct mammals. The bones in the upper stalagmite floor (2), and the cave earth (4), have been split open longitudinally, evidently by man for the marrow, and have been gnawed apparently by hyenas. In this stalagmite, near its base, was a human jaw-bone. The black band (3) is of circumscribed dimensions, occupying about one hundred square feet, and is composed of charred wood to the depth of from three to thirty-six inches. This is considered to have been the portion of the cavern where the cave-men made their domicile. Here, and in the cave earth (4), were found a few bone implements, consisting of an awl, a needle, a pin, and three harpoons. In the older stalagmite floor (5), and the breccia (6), are bones of the cave bear, while those of the later animals, namely, the hyena, elephant, and rhinoceros, are here wanting; and imbedded about three feet deep in the breccia, which is a hard rock-like concrete, was discovered a flint flake, and a chip apparently thrown off in making such a tool, in the neighbourhood of teeth of the cave bear. The flint flake is a testimony of enormous consequence if it affords evidence of human workmanship. The Committee, by careful inspection, have satisfied themselves that such is the case, and, moreover, that it was not possible for the article to have passed down into its rocky bed from any superior and earlier deposit.

The stalagmite floors give indications whereby some

idea of the great age of these deposits may be formed. The deposit is produced by percolations of water passing through the roof, which, on their way, dissolve the lime in the rocks therein, and dripping down lay this on the floor below. The deposit consists of very thin laminæ, which are very slowly accumulated. Happily there are signs by which a computation of the possible time occupied in forming such a coating may be obtained. On a portion of the floor from which the stalagmite was removed twenty-two years ago, at a spot where the drip is abundant, not an appearance of a fresh deposit has yet manifested itself. The cavern has been known and visited from time immemorial, and on a surface of the upper floor, where the stalagmite has reached the thickness of more than twelve feet, are numerous inscriptions of initials, with dates reaching back to the years 1618 and 1615. Notwithstanding that the drip is unusually copious in this part, the film of stalagmite spread over these ancient inscriptions does not exceed one-twentieth of an inch in thickness. Now a rate of progress to that extent only in the course of two centuries and a-half, represents the vast period of 720,000 years for the deposition of this stalagmite. And there is the second floor of even greater thickness, with the intervention of the cave earth between the two, consisting of accumulations gradually made through the outer entrances, and reaching to a depth of twenty feet; and below all lies the breccia, which is of unascertained depth.

It has been the common consolation of those who cling to the Bible as a work of divine origin, that, however much the ground may be disturbed under their feet by the discoveries made of geological deposits with animal remains therein of incalculably remote periods, the proof that man was on the earth before the time marked out for him in the Mosaic account was wanting. This refuge is now taken away beyond hope of recovery, and it is for them to consider what view they can now hold of the disturbed record. The device of stretching the genealogies is of course manifestly insufficient.

I proceed with the evidence of the antiquity of the globe and its animated creation, irrespective of man.

The ages of certain trees are calculated by the number of concentric rings of annual growth ascertainable on cutting them through near their roots. It has thus been estimated that a specimen of the Baobab-tree of Senegal, measuring thirty feet in diameter, must have had a growth of 5,150 years, and that a Taxodium of Mexico, measuring 117 feet in circumference, must have been even more aged (*Lyell's Prin. of Geo.,* II. 44, 45).

The sediment of the Nile was examined at the pedestal of the colossal statue of Rameses, at Memphis, in 1850, by Mr Horner, under the auspices of the Royal Society. The middle of the reign of Rameses, according to Lepsius, would be B.C. 1361. The mud from the lower foundation of the pedestal had accumulated to the height of 10 ft. 6¾ in. Allowing for a certain extended basis of foundation, the calculation is that 9 ft. 4 in. of the now buried portion of the pedestal stood above the surface at the period of its construction. The accumulation of the mud, reckoned for these 3,200 years, was thus at the rate of 3½ inches in a century. The further deposit downwards to the desert sand measured 32 feet, for which an additional period is required of 10,971 years, making a total for the whole deposit of above 14,000 years (*Lyell's Prin. of Geo.,* I. 431-439.)

The Niagara has a fall of 165 feet over a ridge of hard limestone rock. The channel has been cut back by the rush of the waters to the extent of seven miles. This, it is supposed, may have been at the rate of a foot a year, giving a period of close upon 37,000 years for the apparent effects of the fall (*Prin. of Geo.*, I. 358-361).

Professor Agassiz reckons that the growth of the coral reefs of Florida must have occupied 135,000 years (*Lyell's Antiquity of Man,* 44).

The cuttings at New Orleans, in the delta of the Mississippi, made by Dr Bennet Dowler, and before referred to, disclosed ten successive growths of cypress forests over a growth of aquatic plants, the whole being now crowned by a wood of live oaks. For these productions, in replacement one of the other, 158,400 years are claimed (*Types of Mankind,* 337, 338).

These are indications on the surface, or upper crust of the earth, and which, though embracing periods of such magnitude, represent merely modern eras comparatively to the ages required for operations that have left their traces deeper down. There is what is distinguished as the Tertiary period, divided into three great sections, termed Pliocene, Miocene, and Eocene. Then we pass to the cretaceous or chalk-formations. These are wholly made up of remains of marine animals, mostly infinitesimally small, and calculated, when the various deposits are arranged together, to reach in England to the depth of 1,000 feet. After this come other formations, till we arrive at the coal measures, and then we pass to the lowest strata, termed Devonian, Silurian, Cambrian, and Laurentian. Throughout the whole of these deposits traces of plants and living forms are found preserved as lasting memorials of past creations in ages too remote to be even distantly estimated. Sir Charles Lyell hazards the supposition that to the Cambrian, which is not the lowest formation, may be attributed 240 millions of years (*Prin. of Geo.*, I. 340).

Astronomical results throw great light upon this branch of testimony.

There are cycles of time, patent to every one, which are marked by movements of the earth and its satellite the moon. There is the diurnal cycle of twenty-four hours given by the rotation of the earth on its axis; the lunar cycle of twenty-nine days and a fraction caused by the moon's passage round the earth; and the solar cycle of 365 days and a fraction, being the time occupied by the earth in its orbit round the sun. These cycles proceed by a steady uniform progression to complete themselves, and are repeated *ad infinitum*. They have also their uses. The diurnal cycle gives us seasons of activity and of repose. The lunar changes affect the human constitution and the tides. The solar cycle brings with it the alternation of the seasons. And there are more extended cycles which, it is fair to presume, have the same characteristics; that is, a uniform rate of progress to a completion; and then repetitions; and, furthermore, their uses.

I have already spoken of the precession of the equinoxes as a movement of the great duration of 25,810 years. It has an ascertained rate of progress, and, if I have read aright the ancient zodiacs of Egypt and India, it has been brought to a completion, with recurring progress. This movement appears to be one effecting climatic changes.

The earth has its passage round the sun, not in the

form of a circle, but of an ellipse, which is moreover
constantly altering in its proportions. The orbit is
out of eccentricity, that is out of the true circular
form, by distances ranging at the lowest at half a
million of miles, and at the highest at fourteen millions.
The eccentricity now measures three millions of miles,
and according to calculation made by Mr Stone of
the Greenwich Observatory, it will take 210,065 years
to bring the orbit eleven millions of miles onwards to
its greatest eccentricity (*Lyell's Prin. of Geo.*, I. 292).
For the two and a half millions of miles from its present point to the point of lowest eccentricity, will
require, at the same rate, 47,740 years, making a
period for the total movement of 257,805 years.
And it would occupy as much more to bring the
orbit back from its highest to its lowest eccentricity. Thus for this movement we appear to have a
cycle of 515,610 years.

The precession of the equinoxes, I have explained,
is caused by a slow circular movement of the poles of
the earth. Mr J. E. Mayall, in a paper on " Volcanic
Theories" read by him in January 1870 before the
Naturalists' Society of Brighton, mentions the important circumstance that this movement is not in a true
circle, but is spiral, the points of the circle not meeting, but passing each other by, he represents, four
degrees. Mr Mayall designs to enlarge upon this
subject in a future publication, and assures me that
his fact, though not given in any of the astronomical
manuals, is one that will not be disputed by astronomers of the day. Mr Mackey's treatise on Mythological Astronomy, published in 1827, has this
same movement (72, 73, 111, 112), and it is used by
him in calculating the lengthened periods of the

Hindus, to whom he attributes a knowledge of the phenomenon. For example, a change of four degrees at every precessional revolution would involve ninety such changes to complete the circle of 360 degrees, and the Maha-yuga of the Hindus, being 1,080,000 sidereal years, Mr Mackey considers to be made up of forty-five such passages, or the half of the great cycle they would represent in their totality, the Hindu calculation for the precessional movement being here taken at 24,000 years.

Accepting the statement that the revolution of the poles now in question is spiral in form, as stated by Mr Mayall, its effect would be a continuous alteration of the position of the poles. My diagram No. 4 is to describe the spiral movement. Taking one of the poles to be at " P," as it passes round, in effecting the precession of the equinoxes, it arrives lower down at " p." And as this movement proceeds, the poles would perform a complete revolution, as expressed in my diagrams 5 to 8. That is, placing the north and south poles vertically, as in diagram 5, after one precessional revolution they would pass to the position of the inclined dotted line "n s;" they would in time become horizontal as in diagram 6; after that they would in progress of time be reversed, as in diagram 7; then again become horizontal, as in diagram 8; and, finally, pass on to resume their first position, as in diagram 5. In other words, the poles would gradually pass from the arctic and antarctic regions to that of the equator; they would then reverse themselves; then again pass into the place of the equator; and finally go back to their original position.

The angle of the equator with the ecliptic is undergoing continual alteration. " In the Surya-Sidhanta," says Higgins, " Meya, the great astronomer, has stated

the obliquity of the ecliptic in his time at 24°." " Both
the Greeks and Romans," he adds, were aware "that
the angle of the equator and ecliptic has been decreas-
ing from the earliest time" (*Anac.* I., 203, 789). The
angle at the present time measures 23° 28.' Ptolemy
(A.D. 150), Mr Mayall states, gave it as 23° 51' in his
day. The diminution observed by modern astronomers is at the rate of forty-eight seconds in a century.
Sir John Herschel considers the movement to be
caused by the influences of the surrounding planets
altering the plane of the earth's orbit, and that it is
an oscillatory one, limited to a range of less than 1°
21' on each side of a mean position ; and he says that
it is a distinct action from the attraction of the sun
and the moon upon the equatorial region which pro-
duces the precession of the equinoxes (*Outlines of
Astronomy*, 7th ed., pp. 206 *note*, 437, 438). The rotation of the poles mentioned by Mr Mackey, and now
insisted on by Mr Mayall, would involve the combination of these two movements and the continuous
change of the angle. Mr Mackey, in support of his
position, says, "We are told by Herodotus that the
CHOEN, or men of learning in this country (Egypt),
informed him that the pole of the earth and the pole
of the ecliptic had formerly coincided" (*Myth. Astr.* 30).
The extent to which Sir John Herschel would limit
the alteration of the angle embraces a space which, at
the given rate of the alteration, requires a period of
20,250 years. That the movement is one thus limited
is hence a circumstance which there has been no opportunity of ascertaining by actual observation. The
allegation depends upon a number of general but
minute and complicated calculations, and it involves
a supposition, difficult to apprehend, that there are two
sets of disturbing forces, each effecting a separate

operation. Mr Mayall's theory associates these disturbing forces in producing together the great complex movement of which he speaks.

There are geological phenomena which amply support Mr Mayall, and for which, in fact, there appears to be no proper explanation but by attributing them to the alteration in the poles of the earth which he describes. These phenomena demonstrate great changes of climate for which geologists have been unable hitherto satisfactorily to account. The most tangible element introduced into the discussion is the varying eccentricity of the earth's orbit, placing the globe at an ever altering distance from the sun. But, singularly enough, we are nearest to him in our cold season, and furthest from him in our hot one. Mr Croll observes, speaking of investigations by Arago, Poisson, Humboldt, and other astronomers, "the general conclusion arrived at, however, was that the climate of our globe could not be much affected by any change which could take place in the ellipticity of its orbit" (*Paper on Geological Time, published in the Philosophical Magazine for May* 1868). Godfrey Higgins' perceptive mind suggested to him the very sufficient cause embraced in the movement of the poles I am now occupied with. Speaking of the apparent antiquity of the earth, he says :

"I allude to a time when the angle which the plane of the ecliptic makes, with the plane of the equator, was much larger than it is at this moment; the effect of which would be to increase the heat in the polar regions, and render them comfortable places of residence for their inhabitants. This easily accounts for the remains of inhabitants of warm climates being found in these regions, which they probably occupied before the creation of man. . . . The circumstance of the animals of the torrid zone being found in the high latitudes near the poles, is itself a decisive proof, to an un-prejudiced mind, that the time must have been when, by the passage of the sun in his ecliptic his line of movement was much nearer the poles than it is now, the northern regions must have possessed a temperate climate" (*Anac.* I. 210).

Speaking again on the same subject of the former high temperature in the polar regions, he says:

" The greater angle made by the two planes will rationally account for this, as its decrease will rationally account for the increase of the cold in those regions, and the constant increase of cold in England" (*Anac.* II. 445).

Mr Mayall has formed a like independent opinion.

The climatic changes in different parts of the earth at distant times are of a marked order, and prevailed, as the movement in question would require, over lengthened periods.

Sir Charles Lyell informs us that British fossil shells of the Pliocene strata are such as now exist at the Mediterranean; that those of Italy, of the like era, are such as are to be found in the Indian Ocean; that those of France, of the Upper Miocene period, are like what are now at Senegal on the west coast of Africa; that in Switzerland, in strata of the same period, have been found fossil plants of which 266 are sub-tropical and 85 tropical; that in Iceland, in the Lower Miocene strata, occur fossil palms, "closely allied to the date-palm," and about eighty other plants of a sort "which would be cut off by such a winter as now prevails in central and southern Europe;" also three crocodiles, and fifteen land and fresh water tortoises; that as near to the pole as our explorers have gone, appear the remains of coniferæ, poplars, willows, beech, oak (some with leaves half a foot long), plane-tree, walnut, plum, buckthorn, and various evergreens, the "large leaved trees" implying "a high summer temperature, while the evergreens exclude the idea of a very cold winter" (*Prin. of Geo.*, I. 199-203).

Sir Charles proceeds thus:

"That these and other fossil plants from arctic localities really lived on the spot, and were not drifted thither by marine currents, is proved by the quantity of leaves pressed together, and in some cases associated with fruits, also by the marsh plants which accompany them, and by the upright trees with roots which were seen by Capt. Inglefield and by Rink. Still further north, in Spitzbergen, in lat. 78° 56' N., no less than ninety-five species of plants are described by Heer, many of them agreeing specifically with north Greenland fossils. In this flora we observe Taxodium of two species, a hazel, poplar, alder, beech, plane-tree, lime (*Tilia*), and a potomogeton, which last indicates a freshwater formation, accumulated on the spot. Such a vigorous growth of fossil trees, in a country within 12° of the pole, where there are now scarcely any· shrubs except a dwarf willow, and a few herbaceous and cryptogamous plants, most of the surface being covered with snow and ice, is truly remarkable. . . . We cannot hesitate to conclude that in Miocene times, when this vegetation flourished in Spitzbergen, North Greenland, and on the Mackenzie river, as well as Banks Land, and other circumpolar countries, there was no snow in the arctic regions, except on the summit of high mountains, and even there perhaps not lasting throughout the year" (I. 203, 204).

Again, in "the Lower Eocene strata, we find in the London clay of the Isle of Sheppey, fossil fruits of the cocoanut, screw pine, and custard apple, reminding us of the hottest parts of the globe ; and in the same beds are six species of *Nautilus* and other genera of shells, such as Conus, Voluta, and Cancellaria, now only met with in warmer seas. The fish also of the same strata, of which fifty species have been described by Agassiz, are declared by him to be characteristic of hotter climates; and among the reptiles are sea-snakes, crocodiles, and several species of turtle" (I. 205).

"Bones of the hippopotamus, of a species closely allied to that now inhabiting the Nile, are often accompanied in the valley of the Thames and elsewhere by a species of bivalve shell *Cyrena fluminalis*, now living in the Nile, and ranging through a great part of Asia as far as Tibet, but quite extinct in the rivers of Europe" (I. 193).

Then we hear that "the trunk of a white spruce tree was dug up by Sir E. Belcher near Wellington Sound, in lat. 75° 32′ N," and that "the remains of an ancient forest were discovered by Captain M'Clure in Bank's Land, in lat. 74° 48′ . . . Evidence of ancient forests· was found in Prince Patrick's Island, and in Melville Island, one of the coldest spots perhaps in the northern hemisphere" (*On Geological Time by Mr Croll, in Phil. Mag. for Nov.* 1868).

The coal measures are composed of plants often of gigantic growth, conifers, palms, ferns, tree-ferns, club mosses, and araucariæ, requiring long sustained high temperature for their production. Fossils of these formations were found by Captain Parry in Melville Island in lat. 75°. Such have also been met with in Bear Island, lat. 74°36′(*Prin. of Geo.*, I. 225). Lyell here refers to the article on the subject in the "Penny Cyclopædia," to which I have turned. "The coal measures of Newcastle," it is there said, "are of the same age as those of Newfoundland, and even of Melville Island in 75° N. lat." Palms, it is stated, were there, and "Melville Island at one time displayed the noble scene of a luxuriant and stately vegetation." The climate of these arctic regions, it is observed, must have been as hot as equinoctial countries, whereas now in Melville Island there are ninety-four days in the year when the sun is never seen above the horizon. "To admit, therefore, the presence of a tropical vegetation in former days in Melville Island, or Baffins' Bay, seems to carry with it the necessity of also admitting that a change has occurred in the position of the earth's axis of rotation—an assumption," adds the writer on his measure of information, "for which we have no evidence at all."

Such are the marks of a high temperature having prevailed in past times in the present frigid regions. And there is the converse testimony of an arctic temperature having existed in the present temperate zone. Here the signs left behind whereby to judge, though of a conclusive description, are necessarily not so multifold as what springs from tropical growth.

I have already spoken of specimens discovered in the valley of Vezère and the grotto of Aurignac by Mr Lartet, and at Vezère, Dordogne, and Charente, by M. de Vibraye, which show the existence of the reindeer in former times in the south of France. Such indications are so numerous that M. Lartet terms this "the Reindeer period, during which this northern animal extended its range to the foot of the Pyrenees, together with several others fitted for a cold climate" (*Lyell's Prin. of Geo.* I. 176.)

The action of ice in regions now possessing too warm a climate to admit of its prevalence is recognised by all geologists. Large blocks of rock, with smaller debris, have been removed from their parent sources and carried to long distances by some sustaining power for which no explanation presents itself but that they must have been borne along upon glaciers, and surfaces of rock are found polished and scored with lines which it is presumed must have been effected by heavy glaciers grinding their way along and over them. There is one well recognised period of this kind, of which Lyell speaks. He says it occurred anterior to, but close upon the age of the valley drifts and cave deposits I have before had occasion to refer to, and extended so far south as lat. 50° in Europe, and lat. 40° in America. The climate, he continues to say, was, to these latitudes,

"Marked by such intensity of cold, and such an accumulation of ice, as to be quite without parallel in corresponding latitudes in the present state of the globe, whether in the northern or southern hemisphere. Some marine shells of living arctic species, and which no longer frequent the seas of temperate latitudes, have been found in some parts of the glacial drifts of Scotland and North America; so that evidence derived from the organic as well as from the inorganic world conspired to establish the former prevalence of a climate now proper to polar latitudes throughout a great part of Europe. . . . The prevalence of a colder climate at the close of the Tertiary, and in the early part of the Post-tertiary periods, has been derived from two perfectly independent sources of evidence; the first of which may be called inorganic, such as erratic blocks, moraines, and the polishing and striation of rocks; and second, the organic, such as the arctic character of the shells found in the drift of temperate regions" (I. 194-198).

In another of his works he traces these signs in Syria and Sicily as far south as from 38° to 33° N. lat., and mentions that this glacial period was of "vast duration" (*Antiquity of Man,* 323, 365).

"The post-glacial beds of the Clyde contain certain species of shells now extinct in the latitudes of Britain, but which still flourish in the seas of Greenland. The post-glacial era is separated from the present by an immense lapse of time. . . . The post-tertiary deposits in our own islands . . . followed the glacial epoch" (*Address of the President of the Edinburgh Geological Society*, 1864-65).

Mr Croll, in his paper appearing in November 1868, before referred to, enters largely into the subject of the glacial periods, of which he traces more than one.

" We have good evidence of at least three ice periods since the beginning of the Tertiary period—one about the middle of the Eocene period, another during the Upper Miocene period, and the third and last well-known glacial epoch."

Then he shows that the traces of these periods, and especially of the remoter ones, must, in the very nature of the geological deposits, be imperfect. The wearing of the rocks by the passage of glaciers can only be apparent when we have earth surfaces before us.

" But, with the exception of the coal-beds, every general formation from top to bottom was formed under water, and none but the under-clays ever existed as a land-surface. . . . An extreme paucity of organic life is a characteristic of a glacial period. . . . But if there is a deficiency of direct positive evidence of a general glaciation of the northern hemisphere during the Middle-Eocene, Upper-Miocene, and other periods similar to what we know took place during the Postpliocene period, there is, however, abundance of indirect evidence in favour of it."

Mr Croll's theory requires an alternation of heat and cold, and he proceeds to notice the existence of such evidence.

" Here (in the Upper Miocene strata) is a bed of conglomerate, indicating a cold and arctic condition of things when it was formed, with icebergs floating around the place now occupied by the city of Turin, overlain and underlain conformably by strata indicating a subtropical condition of climate . . . When we go back to the Middle-Eocene period, we find the ' flysch,' which bears the marks of having been formed during an ice-period, closely associated with the nummulitic strata, indicating a warm condition of climate. . . . Passing back to the cretaceous period, we find, closely associated with the floating ice in the sea of the white chalk, fossil evidence of a warm condition of climate. And then, if we go back to the Permian period, we find glaciers reaching the sea level in the very centre of England, and other indications of an age of ice, as has been clearly proved by Professor Ramsay. But the fossil remains of the Permian period declare emphatically the prevalence of a warm and equable condition of climate also during that age.

Mr Mayall has noticed that the position of the volcanoes corresponds with the movement the earth undergoes in effecting the precession of the equinoxes. This, he has said, is a spiral rotation, and in just such pericycloidal curves as describe it, the volcanoes are found to run round the earth's surface. M. de Beaumont has similarly observed that the volcanoes are thrown up in " one uniform direction, being parallel to each other within a few degrees of the compass," and while controverting his views, Sir Charles Lyell allows that there are " nine parallel chains in France, Germany, and Sweden " (*Prin. of Geo.*, I. 122, 129). Mr Mayall makes out at least twenty-two such lines. Here is a coincidence that can scarcely have been fortuitous. So constant a repetition, on such a scale, of the same phenomenon, cannot, it may be assumed, have occurred, but under some special governing cause. And where there is a rotatory movement of the earth corresponding with the invariable line of the projection of the volcanoes, the two may fairly be associated together. The line, it may consequently be inferred, is that represented by the ecliptic, not in the fixed form in which the ecliptic is currently drawn, but pericycloidal, passing in repeated curvatures round the globe from one pole to the other. It is on this line that the earth is brought vertically under the action of the sun, whose potent influences, in some manner yet to be made clear, facilitate, it may be thought, the projection of the molten matter, circulating within the earth's crust, by the fissures, or passages, constituting the volcanoes.

Mr Mayall has satisfied himself of the special form of the precessional movement, and, at the same time, of the rate at which this brings about the rotation of the earth on its poles, by comparing the present position of the star β Arietis with the place at which Meton reports it to have stood in his day, B.C. 450, making out, by the system of recurring curves, that the line of the special progress in question deflects from a true circle by just four degrees at each precessional revolution. Meton was a Greek astronomer of repute, deriving his knowledge from the more ancient masters in Egypt, but the means of observation at that remote period were rude, and the measure of progress being, moreover, a round one, its perfect accuracy may be questioned. It is obviously safer, and even proper, to adopt the well ascertained rate at which the angle of the ecliptic with the equator is undergoing alteration, this being evidently a consequence of the movement. Taking then, notwithstanding the great authority standing on the other side, the change in the angle to be a continuous one, we arrive at the enormous period of 2,700,000 years occupied by the globe in effecting a complete revolution of its poles. This cycle, like all the lesser ones, has the characteristics of a fixed scale of progression, of completing itself with repetitions, and of producing marked consequences materially affecting the condition of the earth.

I proceed now to calculate the measures of time involved in the data which I have been describing.

There are, as it has been seen, fossil plants, shells, and carboniferous formations, the products of the temperate and torrid zones, which have been found as far north as lat. 74° 48′, 75° 32′, and 78° 56′. It would not be too much to claim for these transferences, so to call them, a passage over 56 degrees of the circle, which would bring the original regions of the fossils to from 19 to 23 degrees from the present position of the equator, representing, at the rate of the alteration of the angle of the ecliptic, the period of 420,000 years.

Then, if there are at the least twenty-two chains of volcanoes, each marking a passage onwards of the ecliptic, there is involved as many revolutions of the equinoxes, or 567,820 years.

The Committee of the British Association engaged with the examination of Kent's Cavern have been at a loss to account for the formation of the two distinct floors of stalagmite there existing. These are ordinarily separated by the interposed cave earth, but there are places where the two floors approach each other and come in contact, and yet are distinguishable. I am informed, from a competent quarter, that the same remarkable phenomenon occurs in the French and Belgian archæological caves. The circumstance is thus referrible to some general cause, and is not to be explained by any of a local description, even were it possible to conceive such adequate local cause.

The revolution of the poles, of which I am treating, affords the sufficient solution. It is evident that the flooring of stalagmite would be continuous so long as the drip depositing it might continue. Something then must have arrested the drip, and this for a long continuance of time. The congellation of the aqueous sources by the intervention of a glacial period would bind it up, nor is it conceivable that there can have been any other sufficient cause to put an end to the percolations, and then permit of their resump-. tion. The lower floor would be formed while the portion of the globe in which the cavern is situated was in a temperature admitting of the aqueous drip; the drip would cease when the locality passed into an arctic temperature; and then, on its moving onwards into a warm climate, the flow would be resumed, and the second flooring deposited. I will assume that the glacial region may be represented by 20 degrees marked on either side of the north pole. Torquay being about 20 degrees short of this point, 60 degrees have here to be deducted from the 360 degrees of the circle, leaving 300 degrees over which the locality in question must have passed, measuring from the beginning of the formation of the first floor of stalagmite to the present surface of the second floor. For this, at the stated rate of progress, the enormous period of 2,250,000 years is required. The estimate I have hazarded of the time requisite for the accumulation of the upper floor by drip, corresponds with this astronomical time, falling, however, below it. For the 120 degrees, namely from lat. 70° south to lat. 50° north, during the passage over which space the upper floor may have been formed, 900,000 years would be required, while the estimate I have made

for the drip is 720,000.   With more accurate data the
periods, it is quite conceivable, might be brought into
closer accord.   For instance, the glacial period might
be shorter than I have stated it, and the season of the
drip proportionately lengthened ; or, if the drip were at
the rate of the twenty-fifth of an inch, in lieu of a
twentieth, in the two centuries and a-half during which
its progress is observable, the calculations would
agree exactly.   In the phenomena then of Kent's
cavern we appear to have the highest evidence yet
obtained for man's antiquity, requiring that the
measure of his time on earth should be expressed, not
in thousands, but in millions of years.

The time when the North Pole was in a warm region, as marked by the fossils which have had their
growth there, and that when ice prevailed in the present regions of warmth, denote one and the same
position of the earth when these phenomena occur at
the same geological stratum or earth surface, but when
the earth surface where either of them appears differs,
there evidence is given of a distinct revolution of the
globe. I make out, in this manner, eight such revolutions.

1. The glacial epoch at the close of the Tertiary
period.

2. Fossils of the Pliocene period found in the Arctic
zone.

3. Do. of the Upper Miocene period.

4. Glacial epoch of the Middle Eocene period.

5. Fossils of the Lower Eocene period found in the
arctic zone.

6. Glacial epoch of the Cretaceous period.

7. Do. of the Permian period.

8. Fossils of the Carboniferous period found in the
arctic zone.

And to these must be added another, called for by
the two-fold stalagmite flooring of Kent's Cavern
occurring in the Post Tertiary period. The nine rota-
tions give the enormous period of 24,300,000 years
apparently registered upon the earth's crust.

But my list is obviously an imperfect one. The
Cretacious and Permian periods are far removed from
each other, and with six revolutions marked at the
strata lying above the former, there must have been
several such revolutions in those intermediate to them.
The coal measures in themselves present a very great
range, interrupted by extensive deposits of shale and
freestone, involving vast ages and changes of climature.
Sir Charles Lyell speaks of glacial operations connected with these deposits :—

"Among the mammalia occurring in the same carbona-
ceous shales are an elephant (*E. antiquus*), an extinct species
of bear (*Ursus spelæus*), and a rhinoceros different from
R. tichorhinus. That the formation of the shale and lignite
containing the above-mentioned remains was preceded and
followed by periods of greater cold, is shown by the polished
and striated rock surfaces, on which the lignite rests, and by
the large size of the erratic blocks which are superimposed
upon the lignite" (*Prin. of Geo.* I., 196, 197).

And finally there is a very extensive succession of
ranges to be accounted for from the carboniferous to the
lowest observed stratum, all stocked more or less with
fossils, during the deposition of which these climatic
changes must have occurred. It requires but eighty-
nine recurrences of the great cycle I have been speaking of to produce the 240 millions of years which Sir
Charles Lyell claims as possibly representing the age
of the Cambrian formation, after which there is still

the Laurentian; and it is no strain upon the proba-
bilities to concede the period, vast though it be.

We are associated with other great cycles the occurrence of which supports the evidence for the connection of our system with high ranges of time.
The comets of 1840, 1847, and 1680, have orbits computed to occupy 13,864, 13,918, and 15,864 years.
That of 1780 requires, it is said, 75,314 years to complete its course; and for those of 1844 and 1744 the
still greater periods of 102,050 and 122,683 years are
given (*Chambers*, 310). And of these circuits there
may be endless repetitions.

In fact, when our eyes are opened to discern something of the dimensions of the works of the Creator,
measures of time and space are lost in the contact with
infinitude. Light is said to travel at the inconceiv-
able rate of 184,000 miles in a second. The nearest to
us of what are termed the fixed stars, which is one in
the constellation Centaur, is held to be so far off that
even at this prodigious rate it takes three years and
forty days for a ray of light, shed from it, to reach us.
The distance is computed to be about nineteen billions
of miles, which means nineteen thousand thousands of
millions of miles, or nineteen millions of millions. But
this forms but a unit in these measureless calculations.
There are stars, those of the sixteenth magnitude, so
remote as to require, it is thought, 5,620 years for their
light to have reached us. My figures are taken from
Chambers. Nor is this all. Beyond the ascertained
astral forms, there are nebulous clouds, apparently
composed of gaseous bodies, but which possibly may
have the characteristics or spheres of stars, and with
spaces allotted to them adequate for independent
action; and there are filmy spots beyond these, which

may be of the same character, existing at infinitely removed further distances.

And there are, possibly, vast centralizations, grouping together many, or all the systems, requiring orbits and measures of time which the mind of man cannot even approachably imagine. Our whole solar system, for example, is said to be moving towards a point near λ Herculis, at the rate of 148,400,000 miles a year, prosecuting an enormous circuit upon some undiscernible and inconceivably distant centre.

How dwarfed and absolutely frivolous become the pages of the alleged Moses, when measured with the stupendous records set before us, as his real testimonies, by the author of the universe!

Genesis 1:1

Genesis 1:14-19

Psalm 102:25

Isaiah 40:21-24

Job 37:18

Job 38:8-11

Jeremiah 10:12

II Peter 3:5

CONCLUDING OBSERVATIONS.

THE character of the work on which I have occupied myself is sufficiently apparent. It is brought out, in defence of a system, by official advocates. It professes to be an exhibition of divine truth, but the divinity of the alleged truth is assumed, and not in any way sifted, explained, or established. The very task that had to be performed for the silencing of objectors is thus evaded. Why has this been so? Thirty-seven men of cultivated minds, and accustomed to polemical discussions, cannot have one and all failed to see what the demands upon them of the objecting portion of the community really are. Why did they not with fairness and fulness meet their adversaries? The answer is as evident as the failure. They can have had no design of really meeting them. They shrink apparently from the encounter. What they have set themselves to do is to tranquillize the minds of friends, disturbed by the adversaries, with what may plausibly satisfy them. It is another coat of plastering laid upon the crevices of their sacred edifice. My aim has been to unmask the performance.

The Hebrew history, taking it on its own terms, exhibits the people as in a low and miserable state during the times of the judges. They consisted of disconnected tribes, in constant hostilities, struggling for existence, without ordered rule, "every man doing that which is right in his own eyes." At length they

chose for themselves a king, but were still so back-
ward in the arts of life that the ruler and his son
alone possessed such weapons as a sword and spear,
and among them was no artificer capable even of
setting in order their agricultural implements. Could
a people so circumstanced have imparted knowledge to
others ? or would they not be dependent on others for
what they might themselves be able to take up? At this
time their neighbours the Greeks, Chaldeans, Persians,
and Egyptians, had organized governments, and
methodized religious institutions, with the measure of
knowledge in literature, arts, and sciences proper to
such condition. Our comparison relates to a period
removed by 350 years from the age of Moses. Then,
about 650 years later, in the times of Ezra and
Nehemiah, we have the first promulgation of that
work accepted as their oracles from God. What the
cultivation of the Egyptians was, through years long
past, as exhibited in their remains, we have already
seen. The Chaldean advance is shown by those
tokens of knowledge, skill, and grandeur, which have
been unearthed by M. Botta and Mr Layard. The
relics at Behsitoun and Persepolis demonstrate similar
progress on the part of the Persians. And with the
Greeks, the youngest of these nations, we reach the
palmy days of their literature, producing Pythagoras,
Thales, Anacreon, Pindar, Æschylus, Sophocles, Herodotus, Euripides, Thucydides, Socrates, and others of
lesser note.

It is at this time that the Bible, so far as then
made up, is brought to public view under the auspices
of Ezra. His hand over it is recognized by our commentators. In its pages they acknowledge the incor-
poration of traditions such as existed among the

neighbouring nations. The important legends of the
creation, fall, and deluge, so prevailed. Sacrificial
rites, and the initiatory operation of circumcision,
were likewise in common observance around. Other
features, such as the ark, the cherubim, the priestly
order, the Urim and Thummim, the distinction between clean and unclean meats, the priestly costume,
the method of sacrificing, and many different appointed
usages, it is allowed, were adopted by the Hebrew legislator from Pagan models. Did he stop there? Could
he, while so copying, have derived the legends in question, the sacrificial device, and the institution of circumcision, from an independent source? Our commentators strive so to make it out. They cannot
avoid the acknowledgment that the heathen around
had all these things. They seek, therefore, to give to
all some origin that may be respected. The legends
may have been transmitted to all through the channel of the patriarchs. The narrative of the deluge
may be in the very "syllables" of Shem. Sacrifice
comes from a divinely conferred primeval instinct.
Joseph may have indoctrinated the Egyptians in the
advantages of circumcision. What surmises, especially this last! Joseph applying the signet of election to the adversaries of the people of God! Could
demonstrations be more plainly given of the weakness of the cause? and of the resolution to maintain
it notwithstanding all opposing testimony? System
must be made to stand. Truth does not attract the
like attention. But, after all, do we get what we have
to look for, a record passed on to us pure from Moses,
as communicated to him by God? That position is
irrecoverably abandoned. If he copied from the
heathen that which he is allowed to have adopted

from their models, the tie of the divine inspiration so far disappears. And if he framed his narratives upon floating traditions, to whomsoever traceable, it equally vanishes. And if, in so acting, in so providing his materials from existing human sources, he tells us that he got them by direct communication from the deity, what becomes of his integrity? And it is thus our commentators leave the Bible, exhibiting it, in all essentials, with the traces of human origin, while professing to accept it as altogether divine.

The battle, therefore, with the critics is lost at the very threshold of these discussions.

The next contest is with the men of science. Here our commentators fairly turn their backs and leave the field. The records of the rocks they will not face, and against the array of remorseless facts to prove the antiquity of the human race, their shield of protection is the elasticity of the genealogies. The Mosaic account must be shown to be defective in order to prove it right.

The divine governance of Jehovah called for observation. There is no part of the scripture more constantly, more directly, and more forcibly exciting offence and dissent than the legislation and judgments attributed to him. In the attributes of honesty, truthfulness, chastity, firmness, consistency, impartiality, clemency, justice, and mercy, the creature is seen to stand in nature far above the portrayed creator. Could a reasonable defence have here been offered, we should doubtless have had it.

Miracles and prophecies claimed attention as divine supports, weighty of effect if only true. Here again the duty of defence was too riskful to be undertaken.

This position is abandoned if one of the most notable of these exhibitions is to be accepted on the impressions of a Pagan prophet of a phenomenon which had no real existence.

And then we come to the department of history. The exodus was from out of an ancient and highly cultivated nation, having ample records. The passage was to territories tributary to them. Not a word appears about the Hebrew race throughout the Egyptian annals. The renowned patriarch, the founder of the stock, visits the land, and receives honours from their king. His great-grandson Joseph administers their affairs through a long series of years, preluded by divine manifestations. The whole family migrate thither, and speedily swell to the proportions of a nation. Moses is trained in the royal household, and then proves a defiant rebel. Armed with direct power from above, he showers fearful visitations, time after time, upon the land and its inhabitants. He takes his people out from the hands of their terror-stricken oppressors, and when the king revives from his fears, and follows them with his hosts, he overwhelms the whole, by a miraculous operation, in the waters of the Red Sea. At length the lands of their divinely conferred inheritance are entered, and combat after combat, with awful indiscriminative slaughterings, gives them a measure of possession. And this land, as I have already noticed, is tributary to the Egyptians, their domination spreading over it and beyond it to Syria and Chaldea. It is a certainty, that had these events really occurred, some notice of them must have appeared in the monumental registries and well-kept records of the Egyptians. Our commentators show but too much consciousness that this should be so, and vainly struggle, but without an atom of success, to associate the two people together in their histories. Beyond the miraculous narratives for which independent proofs are requisite, we have not a single particle of the to be expected information. The Hebrews say not one word of the Egyptians, and the Egyptians know nothing of the Hebrews. The painful attempts the commentators make to exhibit an association of the sort required, only serve to show that none has existed. This was a support which the Bible could assuredly have had, and it has it not.

The value of the failure to the advocates, not of system, but of truth, is inestimable. What those involved in system will say thereto is unfortunately another matter.

Turnbull and Spears, Printers, Edinburgh.

CPSIA information can be obtained
at www.ICGtesting.com
Printed in the USA
BVHW042046291118
533410BV00022B/187/P